序

　　自民國六十三年"中國餐點"出版以來，雖經過了漫長的歲月，仍廣受讀者們的愛顧，還在不斷的銷售中。10年來各方面都有長足的進步，由於精密儀器的發展，照相、印刷素質的提高自不待言，甚而日常使用的烹飪材料也多科學化了。如米製品，以往需先將米磨成米漿後才能使用，而現在市面上已有磨好的米粉包裝成袋出售。

　　為配合社會的進步與大眾的需要，我們決定將原有的食譜重新調整，除將內容再一次的選擇外，也將食譜再試驗，力求簡單、效率化，並以中英文版發行，便利海內、外讀者使用。

INTRODUCTION

Eleven years have passed since CHINESE SNACKS was published and I am pleased that it is still as popular internationally as it is in Taiwan.

Recent scientific research and technological developments have influenced all our lives. The food industry has been changed greatly. Many of the ingredients used in food preparation are now produced more scientifically, and are more readily available.

Not too long ago, we had to grind rice to make rice paste. Now, we can purchase readymade rice flour and all we have to do is mix it with water to make rice paste. The high quality of the photographs and printing of our books are produced by state of the art equipment and materials.

I decided to revise CHINESE SNACKS to update and simplify the directions and, in some cases, to provide the use of new and different ingredients. This edition also includes step-by-step photographs that enable you to prepare Chinese snacks more easily, efficiently, and economically. The recipes have been tested several times in Wei-Chuan's kitchen to insure their accuracy and the directions have been carefully edited.

Chinese Snacks is published as an English-Chinese bilingual edition to meet the needs of the people in Taiwan and to continue to assist English speaking people in the art of Chinese food preparation.

Wei-Chuan's Cooking extends an invitation to the neophyte to delve into the art of preparing Chinese Snacks.

Comments and recommendations regarding this book are most welcome.

Huang Su Huei

點心專輯 Chinese Snacks

做中國點心除應俱備菜刀、菜板、鍋鏟、漏杓、炒鍋等用具外，仍需有量杯、量匙、篩子、趕麵桿、打蛋器及蒸籠等特殊用具。

Besides cleaver, chopping board, spatula, strainer and wok; utensils such as cup, tablespoon, teaspoon, sifter, rolling pin and electric mixer (or wire whisk) are also used to prepare Chinese snacks.

量杯、量匙：做點心不比做菜，其份量的控制十分重要，例如：和麵粉時加入的水、蛋、奶水等份量如果不準確，則揉出的麵糰不是太軟就是太硬，因此點心往往做不成功。而麵粉又因地區或廠牌的不同其濕度也有差異，即同份量的麵粉需要加的水份卻不盡相同，所以在製作點心時，除了參考書本上所提供的份量外亦需利用自已日常製作麵點的經驗，才能得心應手做出美味的點心。

Cup, tablespoon and teaspoon: measuring ingredients is very important in making snacks. Failure to measure ingredients correctly is the main reason for unsuccessful results. Using the incorrect amount of water, eggs or milk will cause the dough to become too dry or too moist. The amount of water used to make leavened dough varies because the moisture in the flour is different from region to region and from brand to brand. The reader may refer to this book for the correct measurements or may change them, if necessary, according to personal experience in making delicious snacks.

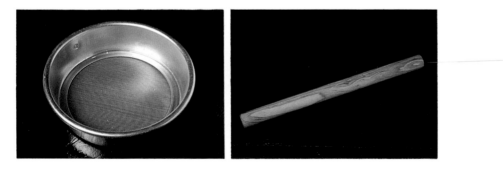

篩子：做點心時使用篩子的機會很多，其用意是：
1. 麵粉或發粉易結顆粒，經篩過後粉質膨脹細膩。
2. 有數種粉類需要混合時，將其過篩，不但除去結粒，更使其混合均勻。

趕麵桿：揉好的麵糰要趕成長條或薄片時，都要利用到趕麵桿，趕麵桿有長有短，有粗有細，可依個人使用的習慣選用。

Sifter: The sifter is essential in making snacks. It is used to pass flour, or any other dry mixture, through it. Sifting allows air to pass through the flour and breaks up any lumps. The sifter is also used to evenly mix different ingredients. Sifted flour should be spooned lightly.

Rolling pin: The rolling pin is used to roll out dough. There are many different kinds of rolling pins, select the one that works best for you.

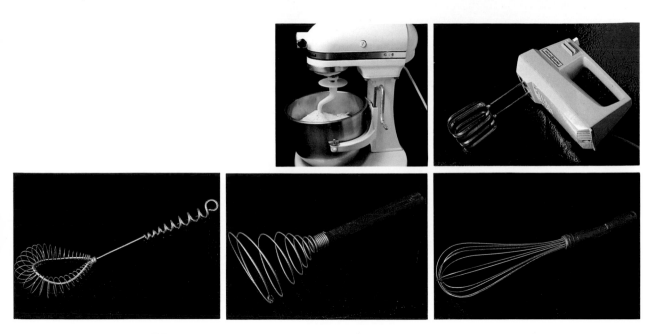

打蛋器：做蛋糕時常常要用到打蛋器，把蛋打發，打蛋器種類計有：手動打蛋器、半自動打蛋器、全自動打蛋器，不論那一種都可使用。

Electric mixers: A stationary or hand held mixer may be used to mix or blend ingredients.
Wire whisk, hand beaters: These utensils may be used to whip or beat ingredients. Although these utensils are easier to use, they require more energy and time.

蒸籠：做中國式點心不免要用到蒸籠，傳統式的蒸籠是竹製的，有其優、缺點：
優點是密封，可保持一定的熱度，不易滴水。缺點是體積大，使用時下面還要墊一鍋盛水，易燒焦損壞，不易收藏且國外較不易買到。
國外常見的西式電鍋，可以利用做為蒸器，只要在鍋內加水，放上一個放食物的鐵架，就是個理想的蒸器了，但缺點是，火力略嫌不足。
凡是蒸生的食物、包子、饅頭或蛋糕等，最重要的是一定要先將水燒開，才將食物放入蒸籠或蒸器內，如此熱力夠強，才能蒸的好，否則吃起來會覺黏膩。

Steamer: The traditional Chinese steamer is made of bamboo. It spreads the heat evenly and the steam does not escape during steaming. However, It is impractical for many reasons. It is very large, damages easily, and is not easy to store.

Electric roasting pan, This pan may be used as a steamer. Place a rack in the pan and add water. The disadvantage of using this method of steaming is that the heat is not hot enough. The most important step in steaming is to boil the water before putting the snacks in the steamer. This helps to keep the heat high during steaming and prevents the snacks from becoming "doughy".

凡製作饅頭、包子類都需先發麵，個人發麵方法不同，現歸二類來提供讀者參考。讀者按食譜自行研習實驗，綜合各法之心得選擇自己認為最好的發麵法。

發麵(一)

特點：做法簡單較適合家庭製作，發好的麵泡較大。

麵粉‥‥‥‥‥‥‥‥‥‥‥‥‥‥6杯
① 糖‥‥‥‥‥‥‥‥‥‥‥‥¼杯
溫水‥‥‥‥‥‥‥‥‥‥1¾杯
酵母‥‥‥‥‥‥‥‥‥‥¾大匙
發粉‥‥‥‥‥‥‥‥‥‥1大匙
豬油‥‥‥‥‥‥‥‥‥‥‥‥2大匙

❶ 先將①料內之糖放進溫水內，待溶化撒入酵母。
❷ 擱置10分鐘，上浮一層白沫。
❸ 麵粉過篩，與豬油、①料一同攪拌，太硬或太軟時酌加水或麵粉。
❹ 用手搓勻，把邊上散落的粉全部揉進麵糰，揉至十分光滑。
❺ 放在盆內，蓋上保鮮膜以免表皮乾硬。置於溫暖的地方約2小時左右，麵糰發到三倍時即可用來做點心。

蒸點心注意事項：

❶ 包好餡的點心要擱置略醒後再蒸（醒時蓋上保鮮膜以免表皮乾硬），醒麵的時間視室溫而定，約10～30分鐘，如醒麵的時間太久，麵皮發的太過，則點心蒸出後會塌下。
❷ 點心要蒸時，應在每個點心底墊上一張白紙，或先在蒸籠內舖上濕布，再放入點心。
❸ 蒸點心要用大火，否則蒸出的點心會黏膩。

To make plain steamed rolls, buns and breads of this kind, it is necessary to begin with leavened dough (basic yeast dough). Although your own recipes may not be the same, the following two recipes offer tested alternatives. You may compare these recipes and experiment with them often then choose the one that works best for you.

Levened Dough I

Specialty: This recipe is easy and best for home cooking. By using this method, the dough will have large air bubbles.

```
      6 c.  flour
    ⎧ ¼ c.  sugar
    ⎪ 1¾ c.  warm water
 ① ⎨ 1 T.  yeast
    ⎩ 1 T.  baking powder
      2 T.  shortening
```

❶ In a bowl, dissolve sugar in warm water then add the yeast (Fig. 1).
❷ Let the liquid stand for ten minutes or until the yeast becomes foamy and floats to the top (Fig. 2).
❸ Sift the flour into a bowl. Add the shortening and ① (Fig. 3); mix well. If the dough is too dry, add water; if too moist, add flour.
❹ Knead the dough with the heels of one or both hands until smooth and elastic (Fig. 4).
❺ Place the dough in a bowl and cover it with a sheet of plastic wrap (Fig. 5). Let the dough rise in a warm place for about two hours until it has trippled in bulk.

發麵（二）

特點：製作方法較複雜，通用於餐館或專門製造業者，發出的麵既細緻又甘美。

① $\begin{cases} 麵種\cdots\cdots\cdots\cdots\cdots 3\ 兩 \\ 水\cdots\cdots\cdots\cdots\cdots\cdots \frac{3}{4}\ 杯 \\ 麵粉\cdots\cdots\cdots\cdots\cdots 2\ 杯 \end{cases}$

碱粉或碱水\cdots\cdots\cdots\cdots 1 小匙

② $\begin{cases} 水\cdots\cdots\cdots\cdots\cdots\cdots \frac{3}{4}\ 杯 \\ 糖\cdots\cdots\cdots\cdots\cdots\cdots \frac{1}{4}\ 杯 \\ 猪油\cdots\cdots\cdots\cdots\cdots 2\ 大匙 \end{cases}$

③ $\begin{cases} 麵粉\cdots\cdots\cdots\cdots\cdots 3\ 杯 \\ 發粉\cdots\cdots\cdots\cdots\cdots 1\ 大匙 \end{cases}$

❶將①料內之麵種加水溶化，再加麵粉搓勻成麵糰。

❷放在盆內，蓋上保鮮膜以免表皮乾硬。放置約8小時左右會發到2～3倍，即成「老麵」。

❸②料置盆內加入碱水（若用碱粉，先加少許水溶化）一同攪勻。

＊老麵若過酸才使用碱粉或碱水，否則不必用。

❹把③料過篩加入②料混合液中，拌勻，太硬或太軟時酌加水或麵粉。

❺倒出麵糰與老麵一同揉成軟硬適中的麵糰即可用來做點心。

■發好的麵隔夜後發酸即成麵種，故每次發好麵可事先留下一塊，待過夜發酸後保存在冰箱以備下次發麵時用，大約可保存一星期。

Levened dough II

Specialty: This recipes is more complicated and is best suited for use in restaurants and specialty shops. By using this method the dough is light and delicate with a delicious flavor.

① $\begin{cases} 4 \text{ oz. dough starter} \\ \text{(see ■ below)} \\ \frac{3}{4} \text{ c. water} \\ 2 \text{ c. flour} \\ 1 \text{ t. baking soda} \end{cases}$ ② $\begin{cases} \frac{3}{4} \text{ c. water} \\ \frac{1}{4} \text{ c. surgar} \\ 2 \text{ T. shortening} \end{cases}$ ③ $\begin{cases} 3 \text{ c. flour} \\ 1 \text{ T. baking powder} \end{cases}$

❶ Dough A: In a bowl, dissolve the dough starter of ingredients ① in water. Add flour (Fig. 1) and mix. Knead it into a smooth dough.

❷ Place dough A in a bowl and cover it with a sheet of plastic wrap (Fig. 2). Set aside in a warm place. Let the dough rise for 8 hours until it has doubled or trippled in bulk.

❸ Place ② in a bowl. If the dough is sour, put baking soda in water to dissolve then add it to the bowl (Fig. 3*); mix well.

❹ Dough B: Sift ③ together (Fig. 4) then add ②; mix well. If the dough is too dry, add water; if too moist, add flour.

❺ Combine dough A and dough B (Fig. 5). Knead them together into a smooth and elastic dough.

■ To make dough starter: save a small piece dough from the leavened dough and let it stand over night to become sour. The starter can be kept for one week if it is refrigerated.

＊ Photo shows Potassium Carbonate Solution that is used as baking soda and is only available in Chinese Markets.

Method to Steam Snacks

❶ Cover the snacks with a sheet of plastic wrap; let the snacks stand for 10-30 minutes depending on the weather. Do not let the snacks stand more than 30 minutes or the dough will fall.

❷ Remove the sheet of plastic wrap. Line a steamer with a damp cloth or pieces of paper, 1½" square, on which to set the snacks.

❸ Always steam snacks over boiling water, over high heat; otherwise the snacks will be doughy.

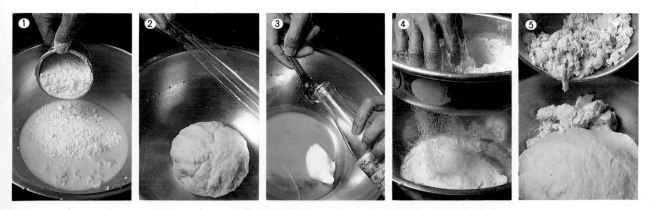

餡：五花肉⋯⋯⋯⋯⋯1斤半　皮：參照第6頁發麵
　　（5公分寬，24片）　　　麻油或沙拉油⋯⋯2大匙
紅葱頭片⋯⋯⋯⋯⋯1大匙　花生粉⋯⋯⋯⋯⋯1杯
　　⎧糖、料酒⋯⋯⋯各1大匙　香菜⋯⋯⋯⋯⋯⋯½杯
　　⎪五香粉⋯⋯⋯⋯½小匙
①⎨水⋯⋯⋯⋯⋯⋯1½杯
　　⎪醬油⋯⋯⋯⋯⋯½杯
鹹菜（切絲）⋯⋯⋯½斤

❶ 餡：油4大匙燒熱，將鹹菜略炒，並加醬油1大匙炒
　　勻盛起。油2大匙燒熱，以中火炒香紅葱頭，呈金黃
　　色時放入五花肉略炒，並加①料燒開，改小火燒煮約
　　40分鐘，再入鹹菜續煮10分鐘即成。

❷ 皮：將發好麵塊揉至十分光滑，太軟或太硬時酌量加
　　水或麵粉，揉成長條並分切成24個小麵糰，每塊壓成
　　直徑12公分之圓餅狀，表面塗抹麻油（圖1），對折成
　　半圓形（圖2），再用手掌輕壓成邊薄中厚的半圓餅
　　（圖3）。

❸ 將筷子底劈開十字深約3公分，插入兩枝牙籤固定，
　　沾上食用色素印在割包上以增美觀，（擱置約10～30
　　分鐘略醒）。水開後放入割包，大火蒸8分鐘至熟即可
　　（參考第6頁蒸點心注意事項）。食時把割包打開依序
　　夾入花生粉、五花肉、鹹菜及香菜等食用。

發好麵糰⋯⋯⋯⋯⋯⋯1份
（參照第6頁發麵）
麻油或沙拉油⋯⋯⋯⋯⋯½杯

❶ 將發好麵糰揉至十分光滑，太軟或太硬時酌量加水
　　或麵粉，揉成長條並分切成12小塊。每一塊趕成長方
　　形薄片，表面塗抹麻油，由一邊捲或由兩邊向中央捲
　　成圓筒狀（圖4），再用筷子或鐵條在中央壓一下（圖
　　5、6），擱置約10～30分鐘略醒。

❷ 水開，放入花捲，用大火蒸12分鐘即成（參考第6頁
　　蒸點心注意事項）。

■ 花捲花樣很多，可隨意變化，也可撒入少許葱花，做
　　成不同款式的花捲。

Taiwanese Steamed Turnovers

Makes 20

Filling:
2 lbs. fresh bacon, cut into 24 pieces (2" wide)
1 T. chopped shallots
⎧1 T. each: sugar, cooking wine
⎪¼ t. 5 spice powder
①⎨1½ c. water
⎪½ c. soy sauce
⅔ lb. shredded pickled mustard cabbage
Skin: See pps. 6, 7, Leavened Dough
　　　2 T. sesame oil or oil
1 c. crushed peanuts
½ c. coriander

❶ Filling: Heat the pan then add 4 T. oil; lightly stir-fry the
pickled mustard cabbage. Add 1 T. soy sauce and
stir to mix well; remove. Heat 2 T. oil; saute chopped
shallots until golden brown. Add the bacon and briefly
stir-fry; add ① and bring to a boil. Cover and turn
the heat to low and cook for 40 minutes. Add the
shredded cabbage and cook for an additional 10
minutes.

❷ Skin: Knead the dough until smooth. If the dough is
too dry, add water; if too moist, add flour. Roll the
dough to a long baton-like roll and cut it into 20
pieces. Flatten a piece of dough to a 5-inch circle
(Fig. 1); brush lightly with sesame oil. Fold the dough
in half (Fig. 2). Lightly press the half circle with the
fleshy part of the hand so that the center is 2¾ inches,
and the edges are thinner than the middle (Fig. 3).
Make the other turnovers in the same manner.

❸ Make two diagonal cuts about 1-inch deep on the
square end of a wooden chopstick. Place a toothpick
in each cuts to separate the 4 sections. Lightly dip
the cut end of the chopstick in red food coloring and
then stamp it on the surface of each turnover. Let
the turnovers stand for 10-30 minutes then steam them
for 8 minutes (see p. 7, Method to Steam Snacks);
remove. Gently open the edges of the turnover and
fill, as desired, with crushed peanuts, filling, and
coriander; eat immediately.

Flower Rolls

Makes 12

dough (see pps. 6, 7, Leavened Dough)
½ c. sesame oil or oil

❶ Prepare the leavened dough. Knead the dough until
it is smooth. If the dough is too dry, add water; if
too moist, add flour. Roll the dough to a long baton-
like roll and cut into 12 pieces. Roll a piece of dough
into thin rectangular shape. Brush with sesame oil; roll
both sides toward the center (Fig. 4); crosswise press
the center with the length of a chopstick (Figs. 5, 6).
Roll the remaining pieces of dough in the same
manner.

❷ Let the rolls stand for about 10-30 minutes then steam
them for 12 minutes (see p. 7, Method to Steam Snacks).

■ Designs for flower rolls vary. Experiment to create
individual designs. A green onion may be added
to create different designs.

發好麵糰··················· 1份
（參照第6頁發麵）
猪油···················· 6大匙

❶ 將發好麵糰揉至十分光滑，太軟或太硬時酌量加水或麵粉，揉成長條並分切成六小塊。

❷ 每份麵塊再分成二等份（外皮及麵心）。
外皮部份：趕成15公分×15公分之正方形薄片。
麵心部份：趕成20公分×10公分之長方形薄片，表面塗抹猪油後，對折成10公分×10公分，再塗一層猪油再對折成10公分×5公分之四層麵塊，然後切成5公分×0.3公分之長條（圖1）。

❸ 把麵心拉長放在外皮中間（圖2），捲成糖菓狀，兩端切斷（圖3），共做六個，擱置約10～30分鐘略醒。水開，放入蒸籠，大火蒸約18分鐘（參考第6頁蒸點心注意事項），吃時可切塊或油炸。

Silver Thread Loaves ("Yin-Sz-Juan")
Makes 6

dough (see pps. 6, 7, Leavened Dough)
6 T. lard or shortening

❶ Prepare leavened dough. Remove risen dough from the bowl and knead it on a floured surface until smooth and elastic (about 5-7 minutes). Roll the dough into a long roll then divide it into 6 pieces.

❷ Divide each piece in half. One half will be dough "A" and the other half will be dough "B".
(A) Use a rolling pin to roll out each piece to a square shape, 6"x6".
(B) Use a rolling pin to roll out each piece to a rectangular shape, 4"x8". Working with dough "B", brush lightly with melted lard or shotening and fold in half. Dough "B" is now 4"x4". Brush lightly with oil; fold in half again. Dough "B" is now 2"x4". Cut this rectangle into 2"x0.1" strips (Fig. 1).

❸ Carefully gather the strips together and stretch them to elongate them then place them in the middle of dough "A" (Fig. 2). Roll dough "A" to enclose the strips. Cut off the two ends (Fig. 3) Follow the same steps to make 5 more loaves. Let the loaves stand for 10-30 minutes then steam them for 18 minutes (see p. 7, Method to Steam Snacks). Before serving, cut the loaves into pieces or deep-fry them.

蒸好麵糰··················· 1份
（參照第6頁發麵）
① { 肥肉（剁爛）或猪油··（3兩）¾杯
　　糖·············（3兩）¾杯

❶ 將①料蒸1分鐘。

❷ 將發好麵糰揉至十分光滑，太軟或太硬時酌量加水或麵粉，均分成二等分。

❸ 把麵糰趕成兩大薄片，將蒸好的①料分別均勻的塗抹在面上，每7公分寬連續折起就成爲每層麵皮中間都有糖漿，切絲，分成24份，每份兩端拉長並盤捲成渦形（圖4. 5. 6.），共做24個，擱置約10～30分鐘略醒。

❹ 水開，放入蒸籠，用大火蒸約12分鐘即可（參考第6頁蒸點心注意事項）。

■ 肥肉需絞兩次或剁成泥狀。

Steamed Snail-shaped Rolls ("Lwo-Sz-Juan")
Makes 24

dough (see pps. 6, 7, Leavened Dough)
① { ¾ c. (3 oz.) ground pork fat* or shortening
　　¾ c. (3 oz.) sugar

❶ Steam ① for 1 minutes.

❷ Prepare leavened dough. Remove risen dough from bowl; knead on floured surface until smooth and elastic (about 5-7 minutes). Divide the dough in half.

❸ Use a rolling pin to roll each half into thin large rectangular shapes. Lightly brush with ①; roll the dough, jelly-roll style, into a roll 2½-inches across. Cut each roll into strips and divide the strips into 24 equal groups. Take each shred group of strips and lightly stretch them until they are about 6-inches long (Fig. 4). Hold one end of the strips between the index finger and thumb. Wind the strips around the fingertips (Fig. 5) and gradually bring fingertips together while winding the rest of the strips. Keep strips even (Fig. 6). Tuck the ends underneath to form snail shape. Shape 23 more snail shaped rolls. Let the rolls rise for 10-30 minutes then steam them for 12 minutes (see p. 7, Method to Steam Snacks). Serve hot.

＊ Pork fat should be ground twice.

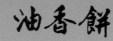

餡：豆沙‥‥‥‥‥‥（1斤）2杯　　皮：參照第6頁發麵

❶**餡**：將豆沙分成24份。

❷**皮**：將發好麵塊揉至十分光滑，太軟或太硬時酌量加水或麵粉，揉成長條並分切成24個小麵糰，用手壓成圓薄皮。

❸每張麵皮，中央置一份餡，包成包子狀。置約10～30分鐘略醒後，放入蒸籠以大火蒸10分鐘即成（參考第6頁蒸點心注意事項）。

豆沙做法

① ｛紅豆‥‥‥‥‥‥‥‥‥12兩
｛水‥‥‥‥‥‥‥‥‥‥8杯　　② ｛猪油（或沙拉油）‥‥‥¾杯
｛糖（10兩）1¾杯

❶豆沙（一）：紅豆加水（滿過紅豆）（圖1）浸泡2小時，倒去水，另加水8杯用大火燒開後改小火煮1½小時至紅豆裂開（圖2），用篩子過濾去渣（如不易過濾可加些水），其汁放入布袋內擠出水份不要，只留豆沙。將豆沙及②料放入鍋內繼續燒煮（煮時需攪拌，不蓋鍋），見水份快乾即成，可做出豆沙1斤4兩。

❷豆沙（二）：做法參照豆沙（一），紅豆煮開後不需過濾，直接加入②料煮（圖3），此法可做出豆沙2斤。

Sweet Buns with Red Bean Paste
Makes 24

Filling: 1¼ lbs. red bean paste
Skin: dough (see pps. 6, 7, Leavened Dough)

❶ Filling: Divide the red bean paste into 24 portions.
❷ Skin: Prepare the leavened dough. Remove risen dough from the bowl and knead it on a floured surface until smooth and elastic (about 5 to 7 minutes). If the dough is too dry, add water; if too moist, and flour. Roll the dough into a long roll, divide it into 24 pieces then flatten each piece with the palm of the hand to form a dough.
❸ Place one portion filling in the middle of a dough and wrap it to enclose the filling. Make the other buns in the same manner. Let the buns rise for 10-30 minutes then steam them for 10 minutes (see p. 7, Method to Steam Snacks). Remove and serve.

Method to Make Red Bean Paste

① ｛1 lb. red beans
｛8 c. water　　② ｛¾ c. lard or oil
｛1¾ c. sugar

❶ Method I: Mix ①, see (Fig. 1). The water must cover the red beans. Soak the beans for 2 hours; drain and discard the water. Add 8 cups water to the beans and bring the water to a boil; cook the beans over low heat for 1½ hours or until they are open (Fig. 2). Strain the beans and discard skins (add water if the beans are too thick to strain). Place the strained beans in a cheesecloth form a pocket and squeeze out the excess water. Put the strained beans and ② in a pan and cook until the water has almost evaporated; stir continously to prevent the bean paste from sticking to the pan. This method yields 1⅔ lbs. red bean paste.
❷ Method II: Follow Method I except omit straining the beans. When the beans are open, add ② to the beans (Fig. 3) and cook until the water has almost evaporated. This method yields 2¼ lbs. red bean paste.

餡：豆沙‥‥‥‥‥‥‥（1斤）2杯
皮：參照第6頁發麵
「炸油」‥‥‥‥‥‥‥‥‥‥‥‥‥‥適量

❶**餡**：豆沙分成24份，搓成圓球狀備用。

❷**皮**：將發好麵塊揉至十分光滑，太軟或太硬時酌量加水或麵粉，揉成長條並分切成24個小麵糰，用手壓成圓薄皮。

❸每張麵皮，中央置一份餡（圖4），包成圓球狀（圖5）再按扁趕成直徑8公分之圓薄餅（圖6），做好之餅置約10～30分鐘略醒（參考第6頁蒸點心注意事項1），放入油鍋內以小火炸6分鐘，再改大火炸1分鐘，呈金黃色撈起即成。

■豆沙做法參照「豆沙包」。

Red Bean Paste Cakes
Makes 24

Filling: 2 c. (1⅓ lb.) red bean paste
Skin: See pps. 6, 7, for Leavened Dough
oil

❶ Filling: Divide red bean paste into 24 portions; roll each portion with the palm of the hand to form balls.
❷ Skin: Prepare the leavened dough. Remove the risen dough from the bowl and knead it on a floured surface until it is smooth and elastic. If the dough is too dry, add water; if too moist, add flour. Roll the dough into a long roll then divide it into 24 pieces. Flatten each dough piece with the palm of the hand into thin circles.
❸ Place one portion of filling in the center of a flattened dough circle (Fig. 4). Wrap the skin to enclose the bean paste completely (Fig. 5); roll it into a ball. Flatten the ball with palm of the hand; use a rolling pin to roll it into 3-inch circle (Fig. 6). Repeat this step for the remaining portions. Let the dough circles stand for 10-30 minutes (see p. 7, Method to Steam Snacks, step 1), Deep-fry the cakes over low heat for 6 minutes; turn the heat to high and fry for an additional minute or until golden. Remove and serve.
■ See p. 13 for directions to make red bean paste.

餡：棗泥⋯⋯⋯⋯（1斤）2杯　　食用紅色水⋯⋯⋯⋯⋯⋯⋯適量
皮：參照第6頁發麵　　　　　　刷子⋯⋯⋯⋯⋯⋯⋯⋯⋯⋯1把

葉子：① { 麵粉⋯⋯⋯⋯½杯
　　　　　水⋯⋯⋯⋯⅙杯
　　　　　食用綠色水⋯3滴 }

❶ 餡：棗泥分成24份，並搓成圓球狀備用。

❷ 皮：① 將①料攪拌並搓成極光滑的麵糰，趕成薄片，切成葉子形狀，需做48片，在其上用小刀背壓上葉脈備用（圖1）。
　　　② 將發好麵塊揉至十分光滑，太軟或太硬時酌量加水或麵粉，揉成長條狀並分切成24個小麵糰用手壓成圓薄皮。

❸ 每張皮中央置一份餡，包成桃形，並將做好的葉子沾水貼在壽桃上。擱置約10分鐘略醒後，水開用大火蒸12分鐘（參考第6頁蒸點心注意事項），取出趁熱在兩葉中間壓一刀痕（圖2），並在其面上噴些紅色（用刷子沾上紅色水，用小刀輕刮刷子面把紅水噴上，圖3）

Steamed Long-life Cakes

Makes 24

Filling: 2 c. (1⅓ lbs.) date paste
Skin: see pps. 6, 7, Leavened Dough
Leaves:
① { ½ c. flour
　　¼ c. water
　　3 drops green food coloring }
red food coloring
brush

❶ Filling: Divide the date paste into 24 portions; roll the date paste into balls.

❷ Skin: ① Mix ① then knead it into a smooth dough. Use a rolling pin to roll the dough into thin sheet. Cut the sheet into 48 leaf-shaped pieces. Use the back of a small knife to make indentation similar to the veins of a leaf (Fig. 1).
　　　② Prepare the leavened dough. Remove the risen dough from the bowl and knead it on a floured surface until it is smooth and elastic. If the dough is too dry, add water; if too sticky, add flour. Roll the dough into a long roll and divide it into 24 pieces; flatten each piece with the palm of the hand to form a thin circle.

❸ Place one portion of the filling in the center of a dough circle; wrap it to enclose the filling. Shape the dough to have one slightly pointed end (similar to a peach). Moisten the back of two leaves with water and attach them to the round (lower) part of the dough ball. Prepare the remaining 23 pieces of dough in the same manner. Let the pieces of dough stand for 10-30 minutes then steam them for 12 minutes (see p. 7, Method to Steam Snacks); remove. Use the dull side of a knife to make an vertical indentation between the two leaves (Fig. 2). Dip a firm brush in red food coloring and run it across the knife to lightly sprinkle the pointed end of each cake (Fig. 3).

餡：雞肉丁⋯⋯⋯⋯⋯⋯12兩

① { 太白粉、料酒⋯各1大匙
　　鹽⋯⋯⋯⋯⋯⋯½小匙 }

蔥、薑末⋯⋯⋯⋯各1大匙

② { 熟筍丁、洋菇片⋯各½杯
　　香菇（泡軟切丁）⋯⋯6朵 }

水⋯⋯⋯⋯⋯⋯⋯⋯¾杯

③ { 太白粉⋯⋯⋯⋯1½大匙
　　料酒、醬油⋯⋯各1大匙
　　麻油、糖⋯⋯⋯各½大匙
　　鹽、胡椒⋯⋯⋯各½小匙 }

皮：參照第6頁發麵

❶ 餡：雞肉丁調①料醃約20分鐘後入鍋炒熟盛起。油4大匙燒熱，將蔥、薑末炒香，隨入②料炒拌並入③料燒開後再加入炒熟雞丁炒勻即可盛盤，待冷備用。

❷ 皮：將發好麵塊揉至十分光滑，太軟或太硬時酌量加水或麵粉，揉成長條並分切成24個小麵糰，用手壓成圓薄皮。

❸ 每張皮中央置1份餡，包成包子（圖4.5.6.）。擱置約10～30分鐘略醒後，水開用大火蒸10分鐘即成（參考第6頁蒸點心注意事項）。

Tasty Chicken Buns

Makes 24

Filling:
1 lb. raw, diced chicken meat
① { 1 T. each: cornstarch, cooking wine
　　¾ t. salt }
1 T. each: chopped green onions, minced ginger root
② { ½ c. each: precooked and diced bamboo shoots, sliced button mushrooms
　　6 pre-softened Chinese black mushrooms, diced }
③ { ¾ c. water
　　1½ t. cornstarch
　　1 T. each: cooking wine, soy sauce
　　½ T. each: sesame oil, sugar
　　½ t. each: salt, pepper }
Skin: See pps. 6, 7, Leavened Dough

❶ Filling: Marinate the chicken meat in ① for 20 minutes. Heat the pan then add oil; stir-fry the meat until it changes color. Heat 4 T. oil; stir-fry the green onions and ginger root until they are fragrant. Add ② and mix; add ③ and bring to a boil. Add the meat and mix well. Remove and allow to cool.

❷ Skin: Prepare the leavened dough. Remove the risen dough from the bowl and knead it on a lightly floured surface until it is smooth and elastic. If the dough is too dry, add water; if too sticky, add flour. Roll the dough into a long roll and cut it into 24 pieces; flatten each piece with the palm of the hand to form a thin circle.

❸ Place one portion of the filling on the center of a dough circle (Fig. 4). Wrap the dough to enclose the filling (Fig. 5). Shape the dough circle by pleating and pinching the edges to form the bun (Fig. 6). Make the other buns in the same manner. Let the buns stand for 10-30 minutes then steam them for 10 minutes (see p. 7, Method to Steam Snacks). Remove and serve.

千層糕　2份

餡：
① 椰茸⋯⋯⋯⋯1½杯　猪油⋯⋯⋯⋯⋯⋯2大匙
　 細糖⋯⋯⋯⋯1杯　紅綠木瓜條⋯⋯⋯⋯½杯
　 奶油(溶化)⋯⋯¼杯　（或其它糖蜜餞）
皮：參照第6頁發麵　玻璃紙⋯⋯30公分×30公分
　　　　　　　　　　（或濕布）

❶ 餡：將①料全部拌勻即為餡，分成8等份。

❷ 皮：將發好麵塊揉至十分光滑，太軟或太硬時酌量加水或麵粉，分切2份。

❸ 每份麵糰趕成40公分×15公分，將1份餡平均撒在中央⅓的面積（圖1），再將左邊⅓折蓋上，再撒上1份餡，最後將右邊⅓折蓋上（圖2），放橫再趕開再撒上餡，如此重覆2次，最後趕成20公分四方塊，下面舖上玻璃紙，上撒紅綠木瓜絲（圖3），置約10～30分鐘略醒後，水燒開，用大火蒸30分鐘至熟（參考第6頁蒸點心注意事項），切塊供食。

Coconut Layer Cakes Makes 2

Filling:
① 1½ c. shredded coconut
　1 c. confectioners sugar
　¼ c. melted butter
Skin: See pps. 6, 7, Leavened Dough
2 T. lard or shortening
½ c. candied papaya shreds
1 sheet plastic wrap (12"x12")

❶ Filling: Mix ingredients of ① and divide into 8 portions.
❷ Skin: Prepare the leavened dough. Remove the dough from the bowl then knead it until smooth. If the dough is too dry, add water; if too sticky, add flour. Cut the dough in half.
❸ Use a rolling pin to roll each half into a 16"x6" rectangular shape. Mentally, vertically divide the rectangular piece into thirds and spread one portion of the filling on the center of the dough (Fig. 1). Fold the left side over the middle; spread with one portion of the filling. fold the right side over (Fig. 2). Turn the folded dough to a horizontal position; repeat the rolling and folding process one more time. Roll out the strip into a 8" square shape. Make the other square in the same manner. Place the square on a sheet of plastic wrap and sprinkle them with papaya shreds (Fig. 3). Let the cakes rise for 30 minutes then steam them for 30 minutes (see p. 7, Method to Steam Snacks). Remove and allow to cool slightly; slice and serve.

小籠包　24個

餡：絞肉⋯⋯⋯⋯⋯½斤　高湯凍⋯⋯⋯⋯⋯¼杯
① 葱末⋯⋯⋯⋯4大匙　皮：參照第6頁發麵份量取其
　雞湯⋯⋯⋯⋯6大匙　　　¼即可
　麻油⋯⋯⋯⋯1大匙
　醬油⋯⋯⋯⋯½大匙
　塩⋯⋯⋯⋯⋯¾小匙

❶ 餡：絞肉加①料攪勻並甩打3分鐘成餡。高湯凍切24小塊。

❷ 皮：將發好麵塊揉至十分光滑，太軟或太硬時酌加水或麵粉，揉好麵塊擱置10分鐘略醒，揉成長條並分切成24個小麵糰，用手壓成圓餅狀。

❸ 每塊皮用趕麵桿，趕成直徑7公分邊薄中間稍厚之圓皮（圖4），把餡置中央，取一塊高湯凍放在餡內（圖5）包成包子（圖6），置約10～30分鐘略醒後，水開用大火蒸8分鐘至熟（參考第6頁蒸點心注意事項），趁熱食用，高湯凍溶化滑潤清香，鮮美可口。

■ 高湯凍做法：雞骨或豬皮加水熬成湯，冷凍即成。或使用膠粉½大匙加雞湯½杯煮開後冷凍。

Little Juicy Steamed Buns Makes 24

Filling:
⅔ lb. ground pork
① 4 T. chopped green onions
　6 T. stock
　1 T. sesame oil
　½ T. soy sauce
　¾ t. salt
　¼ c. jelled stock
Skin: ¼ dough (see pps. 6, 7, Leavened Dough)

❶ Filling: Mix ground pork with ① thoroughly; lightly throw the mixture against inside of the mixing bowl for 3 minutes. Cut the jelled stock into 24 pieces.
❷ Skin: Prepare the leavened dough. Remove the risen dough from the bowl and knead it on a lightly floured surface until it is smooth. If the dough is too dry, add water; if too sticky, add flour. Let the dough stand for 10 minutes; roll it to a long roll and cut it into 24 pieces. Flatten each piece with the palm of the hand to form a dough circle.
❸ Use a rolling pin to roll a flattened dough circle into 3" circle, the middle should be thinner than the edges (Fig. 4). Place one portion of the filling and one piece of jelled stock in the center of the dough circle (Fig. 5). Gather the edges together with the thumb and index finger and form small pleats to enclose the filling (Fig. 6). Prepare the remaining buns in the same manner. Let the buns stand for 10-30 minutes then steam them for 8 minutes. (see p. 7, Method to Steam Snacks). Remove and serve.
■ To make jelled stock: Cook chicken bones or pork skin with water to make soup stock; chill. OR dissolve ½ T. gelatin in ½ cup stock; bring the stock to a boil then chill it.

17

义燒包 24個

餡：叉燒肉……………………12兩　　皮：參照第6頁發麵

① { 糖、醬油、蠔油‥各1½大匙
　　水………………………1杯 }

② { 粟米粉……………………2大匙
　　水……………………2½大匙 }

③ { 猪油……………………2大匙
　　麻油…………………1½小匙
　　胡椒……………………¼小匙 }

❶餡：叉燒肉切1公分四方小薄片（圖1. 2. 3.），把①料燒開加②料煮成濃汁後再加③料即成餡汁，待冷拌入切好肉片即成餡。

❷皮：將發好麵糰揉至十分光滑，太軟或太硬時酌量加水或麵粉，揉成長條並分切成24個小麵糰，用手壓成圓薄皮。

❸每張皮，中央置1份餡，包成包子。擱置約10～30分鐘略醒後，水開用大火蒸12分鐘即成（參考第6頁蒸點心注意事項）。

■叉燒肉做法：參照本公司所出版「實用專輯」第14頁。

Roasted Pork Buns Makes 24

Filling:
　1 lb. roasted pork
① { 1½ T. each: sugar, soy sauce, oyster sauce
　　1 c. water }
② { 2 T. cornstarch
　　2½ T. water } mix
③ { 2 T. lard or shortening
　　1½ t. sesame oil
　　¼ l. pepper }
Skin: See pps. 6, 7, Leavened Dough

❶ Filling: Cook and cut roasted pork into ½" cubes (Figs. 1, 2, 3). Bring ① to a boil. Add mixture ② to thicken, add ③ and mix. Let the mixture cool; add the pork and mix well.

❷ Skin: Prepare the leavened dough. Remove the risen dough from the bowl and knead it on a lightly floured surface until it is smooth and elastic. If the dough is too dry, add water; if too sticky, add flour. Roll the dough into a long roll and cut it into 24 pieces; flatten each piece with the palm of the hand to form a thin circle.

❸ Place one portion of the filling on the center of a dough circle. Wrap the dough to enclose the filling. Shape the dough circle by pleating and pinching the edges to form the bun. Make the other buns in the same manner. Let the buns stand for 10 minutes then steam them for 12 minutes (see p. 7, Method to Steam Snacks). Remove and serve.

■ See p. 14 of "Chinese Cooking for Beginners" for directions to make roasted pork.

素菜包 24個

餡 ① { 高麗菜……………………4杯
　　筍、五香豆乾………各1杯 } 均切小片
　　紅蘿蔔、毛菇………各½杯 }

② { 水………………………½杯
　　醬油…………………3½大匙
　　麻油……………………2大匙
　　太白粉、糖…………各1大匙
　　胡椒……………………½小匙 }

皮：參照第6頁發麵

❶餡：油3大匙燒熱，放入①料炒軟，再入②料炒勻，煮2分鐘後，盛盤待冷備用。

❷皮：將發好麵糰揉至十分光滑，太軟或太硬時酌量加水或麵粉，揉成長條並分切成24個小麵糰，用手壓成圓薄皮。

❸每張皮，中央置1份餡，包成三角包子（圖4. 5. 6.）。擱置約10～30分鐘略醒後，水開用大火蒸12分鐘即成（參考第6頁蒸點心注意事項）。

Vegetable Buns Makes 24

Filling:
① { 4 c. cabbage
　　1 c. each: bamboo shoots,
　　　　　　pressed bean curd
　　½ c. each: carrot, button
　　　　　　mushrooms } cut into small thinly sliced pieces
② { ½ c. water
　　3½ T. soy sauce
　　2 T. sesame oil
　　1 T. each: cornstarch, sugar
　　½ t. pepper }
Skin: See pps. 6, 7, Leavened Dough

❶ Filling: Heat the pan then add 3 T. oil. Stir-fry ① until soft; add ② and mix well. Cook the filling for 2 minutes; remove and allow to cool.

❷ Skin: Prepare the leavened dough. Remove the risen dough from the bowl and knead it on a lightly floured surface until it is smooth and elastic. If the dough is too dry, add water; if too sticky, add flour. Roll the dough into a long roll and cut it into 24 pieces; flatten each piece with the palm of the hand to form a thin circle.

❸ Place one portion of the filling on the center of a dough circle (Fig. 4). Cup the circle in one hand and press two edges together; press the other edges to form a triangular shape and to enclose the filling (Figs. 5, 6). Make the other buns in the same manner. Let the buns stand for 10-30 minutes then steam them for 12 minutes (see p. 7, Method to Steam Snacks). Remove and serve.

麵糰一份：
- 麵粉·········2½杯
- 滾水·········¾杯
- 蛋·········1個
- （或冷水·····¼杯）

麻油·········1大匙

❶ 燙麵糰：滾水沖入麵粉略攪拌，再加蛋或水拌勻，仔細揉成軟硬適度的麵糰，放置20分鐘以上謂之「醒麵」。

❷ 將醒好麵糰置板上，搓成長條狀，分成20小塊，每塊用掌心壓扁（圖1），中間抹油，每二塊疊在一起（圖2），再趕成圓薄餅（圖3）。

❸ 鍋燒熱，（不需抹油）將麵餅置鍋內，以慢火烙烤約20秒，翻面再烙20秒後取出，揭開成兩張荷葉餅。

■ 烙餅時只要把餅烙熟即可，烙好荷葉餅一張張疊於盤內，並用白布蓋住以免冷後變硬。

■ 做好荷葉餅可包捲木須肉或北京烤鴨等來吃。

"Lotus Pad" (Mandarin) Pancakes

Makes 20

Dough
- 2½ c. flour
- ¾ c. boiling water
- 1 egg or ¼ c. cold water
- 1 T. sesame oil

❶ Dough: In a bowl, add boiling water to flour and mix. Add egg or cold water; mix again until smooth. Set aside for 20 minutes. Remove the dough and knead it on a lightly oiled surface until smooth and elastic. Roll the dough to form a long roll and cut it into 20 pieces.

❷ Flatten each piece of dough with the palm of the hand into a 4-inch round piece (Fig. 1); spread lightly with sesame oil. Place two pieces of the dough on top of each other (Fig. 2). Press the round dough pieces together. Roll them out to a 6-inch, thin round dough (Fig. 3). Follow step ❶ for the remaining pieces of dough.

❸ Heat the pan until medium hot; fry the pieces of dough over low heat for about 20 seconds or until small, golden bubbles appear on fried side. While frying, use finger tips to constantly rotate pancakes in a clockwise direction to fry evenly. Turn pancake over and repeat procedure. Remove and separate the pancakes; fold them into quarters and arrange them on a serving plate. Cover with a damp cloth to keep them warm and moist.

These pancakes may be served with "Moo Shu Pork" ("Stir-fried pork and eggs") or with Peking Duckling, green onions, and hoisin sauce.

To reheat the pancakes, steam for 15 seconds and cover with a warm cloth to keep them moist.

燙麵糰·········½份
（參照「荷葉餅」材料）

①
- 蔥末·········1大匙
- 豬油或沙拉油·····½大匙
- 塩·········½小匙

❶ 參照荷葉餅做法❶，做好燙麵糰，放置20分鐘以上謂之「醒麵」。

❷ 將麵糰分成6塊，每塊用手掌壓扁，再用趕麵桿趕壓成圓薄片，撒上⅙的①料（圖4）由兩邊向內折（圖5）再略趕扁，捲成圓筒狀（圖6），平放再趕成圓餅，餅的厚薄隨意。

❸ 油4大匙燒熱，將麵餅煎至兩面呈金黃色取出，也可放入蛋一齊煎。

Chinese Onion Crepes

6 crepes

Dough
- 1¼ c. flour
- ⅜ c. boiling water
- ½ egg or ⅛ c. cold water

①
- 1 T. chopped green onions
- ½ T. lard or shortening
- ½ t. salt

❶ See step ❶ of "Lotus Pad Pancakes". Roll the dough to form a long roll and cut it into 6 pieces.

❷ Use a rolling pin to roll out each piece of dough into a 4-inch round piece. Brush a dough lightly with 1 portion of the shortening of ①, sprinkle salt and green onion (Fig. 4). Fold both sides to the center to slightly overlap (Fig. 5). Lightly flatten and roll over jelly roll style to form the shape of a snail (Fig. 6). Turn the roll on its side and flatten it to a round shape. Follow step ❷ for the remaining pieces of dough.

❸ Heat the pan then add 4 T. oil. stir-fry the crepes until both sides are golden, remove and serve. Eggs may be added to the crepes when stir-frying.

牛肉餡餅 10個

皮
- 麵粉……………2½杯
- 滾水……………¾杯
- 蛋………………1個
- (或冷水…………¼杯)

沾料
- 醬油……………4大匙
- 醋………………1½大匙
- 麻油、辣椒醬各½大匙

餡：牛絞肉……………9兩

①
- 糖………………½大匙
- 麻油……………2大匙
- 水………………2大匙
- 料酒……………1大匙
- 鹽………………¾小匙
- 胡椒……………½小匙

韮菜或葱……………3兩

❶皮：滾水沖入麵粉略攪拌，再加蛋或水拌勻，仔細揉合成軟硬適度的麵糰，放置20分鐘謂之「醒麵」。
❷餡：絞肉調①料，加入切碎的韮菜拌勻，分成10份。
❸將麵糰揉成長條狀，分成10小塊，每塊用手掌按扁(圖1)再趕成圓薄片，包入肉餡(圖2)在摺口處捏緊(圖3)，輕輕按成圓餅狀，全部做好備煎。
❹油3大匙燒熱，放入餡餅，用小火煎約15分鐘至兩面均呈金黃色取出，趁熱淋沾料食用。

Chinese Beef Meat Pies Makes 10

Skin:
- 2½ c. flour
- ¾ c. hot water
- 1 egg or ¼ c. cold water

Filling:
- ¾ lb. ground beef

①
- ½ T. sugar
- 2 T. sesame oil
- 2 T. water
- 1 T. cooking wine
- ¾ t. salt
- ½ t. pepper

Dipping sauce:
- 4 T. soy sauce
- 1½ T. vinegar
- ½ T. each: sesame oil, hot bean paste

¼ lb. green onions
oil

❶ Skin: In a bowl, add boiling water to flour and mix. Add cold water (or egg) and knead into a smooth dough; set aside and let stand for 20 minutes.
❷ Filling: Mix beef and ①; add green onions and mix well. Divide the filling into 10 portions.
❸ Roll the dough into a long roll and cut it into 10 pieces. Flatten each piece with the palm of the hand (Fig. 1). Use a rolling pin to roll each piece of dough into a 4-inch round piece. Place a portion of the filling in center of the dough (Fig. 2); gather the edges of the dough together (Fig. 3) and pinch to seal. Roll the meat-filled dough into a ball and flatten it. Follow the same procedure for the remaining pieces of dough.
❹ Heat the pan then add 3 T. oil; fry the pies over low heat for 15 minutes or until both sides are golden brown. Remove and sprinkle with dipping sauce; serve.

豆沙鍋餅 2份

麵粉……………………¾杯

①
- 蛋……………………2個
- 水……………………¾杯

豆沙、棗泥或蓮蓉…………1杯
「炸油」……………………½杯

❶①料拌勻後，隨入篩過的麵粉，攪拌成糊狀。豆沙分成2份。
❷鍋先燒熱後改小火，用油塗抹鍋面，倒入半份麵糊並轉動鍋子成一大片薄餅(圖4)，豆沙用手壓成四方形(可先在玻璃紙上壓好)再置於餅中央(圖5)，將薄餅兩面向內折起，邊折邊抹上麵糊(圖6)，再將另兩面內折成四方形，順鍋邊加入3大匙油，中火半煎炸至兩面呈金黃色，炸時需轉動鍋子以免燒焦，撈出拭去油份切塊食用。

Red Bean Paste Cake Makes 2

- ¾ c. flour

①
- 2 eggs
- ¾ c. water

- 1 c. red bean paste, date paste, or lotus root paste
- 2 sheets plastic wrap
- oil

❶ In a bowl, mix ① well, add sifted flour and mix into a paste. Divide red bean paste into two portions.
❷ Heat the wok then turn the heat to low; grease the wok with oil. Pour one half of the flour mixture into the wok; rotate the wok (swirl) to form a thin sheet (Fig. 4); remove. Place one half of the red bean paste on a plastic wrap then press it into square. Place the square of red bean paste in center of the flour sheet (Fig. 5); remove the plastic wrap. Fold the sides of the sheet to the center. Spread a little flour mixture on top of the sheet (Fig. 6) then fold the other two sides toward the center to form a square shape. Add 3 T. oil from the edge of the wok; fry the square cake until both sides are golden brown. Rotate the wok during frying to prevent burning. Remove and drain. Repeat this procedure for the other portion. Cut the cakes into pieces; serve.

臘味蘿蔔餅 20個

餡：蘿蔔絲……………1斤
　　臘腸(細丁)………3兩
①{猪油……………3大匙
　麻油……………½大匙
　塩………………1小匙
　胡椒……………¼小匙
「炸油」……………適量

油酥皮：
②{麵粉……………2杯
　猪油……………5大匙
　水………………10大匙
　塩………………¼小匙
③{麵粉……………1杯
　猪油……………5大匙

❶餡：蘿蔔絲加塩1小匙醃15分鐘，擠乾水份。油1大匙燒熱，炒香臘腸盛起待涼。將蘿蔔絲、臘腸與①料拌合即成餡。

❷油酥皮：「水油皮」，將②料拌合成麵糰，揣至極光滑，置20分鐘醒麵後揉成長條，分切成20塊。
「油心」，將③料拌合成麵糰，揣至極光滑，揉成長條，分切成20塊。
「水油皮」包「油心」，(油心不要流出，皮較為酥脆)。包好用手掌壓扁再用趕麵桿趕長(圖1)，捲成筒狀(圖2)，放直再趕長，再捲成筒狀(圖3)，即為「油酥皮」。

❸將做好的油酥皮用手掌壓成直徑8公分之圓麵皮，包上餡，再輕按成直徑約5公分之圓餅，全部包好。
「炸油」燒溫，餅底朝下放入油鍋内(油宜滿過餅⅔處)，用慢火半煎炸約8分鐘，翻面改中火再炸8分鐘至兩面呈金黃色餡熟即成。

Turnip Cakes　Makes 20

Filling:
1 lb. pared, shredded turnips
4 oz. Chinese pork sausage, diced
① {3 T. pork fat
½ T. sesame oil
1 t. salt
¼ t. pepper}
oil

Skin:
② {2 c. flour
5 T. pork fat
10 T. water
¼ t. salt}
③ {1 c. flour
5 T. pork fat}

❶ Filling: In a bowl, add 1 T. salt to shredded turnip, let stand for 15 minutes. Remove and squeeze to remove all water. Heat a pan then add 1 T. oil; stir-fry the sausage for ½ minute. Remove and allow to cool. Mix pork fat, turnip, sausage and ① until thoroughly combined.

❷ Skin: Two separate doughs will be prepared. Dough (A) and Dough (B).
Mix the ingredients of ② together to make a smooth dough (A); knead briefly until very smooth; let stand for 20 minutes then roll into a baton-like roll and cut it into 20 pieces.
Mix together ingredients of ③ to make a smooth dough (B). Roll into a baton-like roll and cut it into 20 pieces.
Flatten pieces of dough (A); place pieces of dough (B) in center of (A) pieces and wrap edges to enclose (B) (To ensure a flaky crust, be sure not to let any part of dough (B) protrude through dough (A)); lightly flatten. Use a rolling pin to roll dough to a rectangular shape (Fig. 1). Beginning at the top edge, roll up the rectangular-shaped dough jelly-roll style (Fig. 2). Turn the piece of dough to a vertical position. Use a rolling pin to roll it to a rectangular shape; roll up the dough again to form a baton-like shape (Fig. 3). Repeat this procedure for all remaining pieces of dough.

❸ Turn rolled dough on its side and flatten lightly; roll it into a 3-inch round piece. Place 1 portion of the filling (1/20) in the center of the dough. Gather the edges to enclose the filling. Pinch to seal. Lightly flatten the filled cakes to form a 2-inch round piece; repeat for all other pieces to make 20 cakes. Heat the oil until medium hot; place turnip cakes in oil, the oil should cover ⅔ of the cakes. Cook over low heat for 8 minutes. Turn cakes over; cook for 8 minutes over medium heat or until golden brown; remove, drain and serve.

咖哩酥餃 20個

餡{絞肉……………12兩
　洋葱丁……………1½杯
　咖哩粉……………3大匙
1{糖……………1½大匙
　塩……………1小匙
　水……………¾杯
2{太白粉……………1½大匙
　水……………1½大匙
油酥皮：
{②料同「臘味蘿蔔餅」
③料同「臘味蘿蔔餅」}

❶餡：油4大匙燒熱，炒香洋葱，隨入咖哩粉略炒，再入絞肉炒熟，加1料燒開，再加2料勾芡，盛出冰涼備用。

❷油酥皮：參照「臘味蘿蔔餅」做法❷。

❸將做好油酥皮逐塊趕成直徑8公分中間稍厚的圓皮，中間包入1½大匙餡，折成半圓(圖4)並將開口捏攏後，用食指與姆指由一端向前折0.5公分捏緊(圖5)，再由捏處的½向前折0.5公分再捏緊(圖6)，如此反覆捏好後，抹上蛋黃。
烤箱先燒熱至375°F，放入咖哩餃烤20分鐘即成。

Curry Meat Turnovers　Makes 20

Filling:
{1 lb. ground pork
1½ c. minced onion
3 T. curry powder}
1 {1½ T. sugar
1 t. salt
¾ c. water}
2 {1½ T. cornstarch
1½ T. water} mix
Skin:
② the same as ingredients ② of "Turnip Cakes"
③ the same as ingredients ③ of "Turnip Cakes"
1 beaten egg yolk

❶ Filling: Heat the wok then add 4 T. oil. Stir-fry onion until fragrant then add curry powder and stir lightly. Add ground pork and stir until cooked; add 1 and bring to a boil. Add 2 to thicken; stir. Remove and let cool.

❷ Skin: See step ❷ of Turnip Cakes.

❸ Roll each piece into a 3-inch round piece (middle should be slightly thick and outside edges thin); place 1½ T. filling in center of dough. Fold dough in half (Fig. 4) and pinch edges to seal. While holding the dough in one hand, use the index finger and thumb of the other hand to fold over the edge about ⅕-inch to make a thin pleat (Fig. 5). Make another ⅕-inch fold at the half way point of this pleat and continue pleating edge (Fig. 6). Continue pleating edge to the opposite edge of dough. Coat one side of the dumpling with a little egg yolk. Repeat this process for each dumpling. Preheat over to 375°F; bake the dumplings, egg coated side up, for 20 minutes; remove and serve.

豆沙酥餅　20個

館：紅豆沙………（半斤）1 杯
「炸油」……………………適量

油酥皮：
① { 麵粉……………2 杯
　　水……………10大匙
　　猪油…………5大匙
　　塩…………¼小匙
② { 麵粉……………1 杯
　　猪油…………5大匙

❶館：紅豆沙分成20份，每份搓圓再輕壓成直徑3公分之圓餅狀。

❷油酥皮：做法參照第25頁「臘味蘿蔔餅」，共做20份。

❸每份油酥皮切成兩半（圖1），每半從切開面壓扁成直徑5公分之圓餅（圖2），把豆沙館夾在中間（酥皮選有線紋面朝外）邊捏緊邊做花樣（圖3）（捏花參照第25頁「咖哩酥餃」圖片説明）。

❹「炸油」略燒熱，放入酥餅用小火炸6分鐘，臨起鍋時改大火炸1分鐘即成。

■紅豆沙做法參照第13頁。

Flaky Red Bean Buns　Makes 20

Filling:
1 c. red bean paste*
Skin:
① { 2 c. flour
　 10 T. water
　 5 T. lard or vegetable shortening
　 ¼ t. salt
② { 1 c. flour
　 5 T. lard or vegetable shortening
oil

❶ Filling: Divide the filling into 20 pieces; roll them into balls. Flatten each balls with the palm of the hand.

❷ Skin: See p. 25, Turnip Cakes, step ❷

❸ Divide each piece of dough in half (Fig. 1). Turn the cut side up, and press each piece to form a 2 inch circular shape (Fig. 2). Place a portion of filling in the center of the uncut side of one of the circles of dough. Place the other circle of dough, cut side out, on top of the filling. Pinch the edges to seal the two dough circles together. Use the index finger and thumb to pleat the outer edge into pleats as shown in (Fig. 3). (See "Curry Dumplings", Figs. of p. 25). Make the other buns in the same manner.

❹ Heat the oil for deep-frying until medium hot; Place the buns in the oil and deep-fry them over low heat for 6 minutes. Turn the heat to high and fry for an additional minute or until they are golden brown; remove, drain and serve.

* See p. 13, "Sweet Buns with Red Bean Paste", for directions to prepare red bean paste.

牡丹花酥　20個

館：紅豆沙………（半斤）1 杯
「炸油」……………………適量

油酥皮：
① { 麵粉……………2 杯
　　水……………10大匙
　　猪油…………5大匙
　　塩…………¼小匙
② { 麵粉……………1 杯
　　猪油…………5大匙

❶館：紅豆沙分成20份，搓圓。

❷油酥皮：做法參照第25頁「臘味蘿蔔餅」，共做20份。

❸每份油酥皮壓成直徑5公分之圓形皮，放入一份豆沙館包成圓球狀（圖4. 5.），用刀在光滑面劃3刀成六等份（圖6）深不可觸及豆沙。「炸油」略燒熱，牡丹花酥切口朝上入鍋，用小火炸10分鐘，待花開改大火炸1分鐘即成。

Sweet Pastry Flowers　Makes 20

Filling: 1 c. red bean paste*
oil
Skin:
① { 2 c. flour
　 10 T. water
　 5 T. lard or vegetable shortening
　 ¼ t. salt
② { 1 c. flour
　 5 T. lard or vegetable shortening

❶ Filling: Cut the red bean paste into 20 pieces; roll each piece into a ball.

❷ Skin: See p. 25, Turnip Cakes, step ❷

❸ Roll each piece of dough into a ball then flatten it to a 2-inch circle; place 1 ball of red bean paste in the center of the dough circle (Fig. 4). Gather the edges (Fig. 5) to completely enclose the filling; pinch the edges securely to seal. To ensure that the sealed dough will not open during frying, roll it around to a smooth surface. Using the sharp edge of a knife (Fig. 6), make 3 diagonal cuts on the smooth side of the dough — do not cut into the red bean paste. Prepare the remaining pieces of dough in the same manner. Place the prepared bean filled dough balls in a strainer or slotted spoon for deep-frying. Heat the pan then add oil. Heat to medium hot; ease the dough balls into the hot oil and deep-fry them over low heat for about 10 minutes or until they "blossom". Turn the heat to high and fry for an additional minute; remove, drain and serve.

* See p. 13, "Sweet Buns with Red Bean Paste", for directions to prepare red bean paste.

餡：①
- 麥芽糖（或蜂蜜）…2大匙
- 糖粉…………………¾杯
- 奶油（先溶化）…2大匙
- 麵粉…………………3大匙

油酥皮：②
- 麵粉…………………2杯
- 猪油…………………5大匙
- 水……………………10大匙
- 塩……………………¼小匙

③
- 麵粉…………………1杯
- 猪油…………………5大匙

❶餡：將①料內之麥芽糖加熱軟化後，加入篩過的糖粉（圖1）並將奶油、麵粉依序加入揉勻（圖2），分切20小塊（圖3）。

❷油酥皮：參照第25頁「臘味蘿蔔餅」做法❷，做成油酥皮，共做20份。

❸將做好油酥皮，逐份壓扁，包上餡，趕成直徑5公分之薄餅，置烤盤上以350度烤20分鐘。

Sunshine Cakes　Makes 20

Filling:
①
- 2 T. honey or maltose
- ¾ c. confectioners sugar
- 2 T. melted butter
- 3 T. flour

Skin:
②
- 2 c. flour
- 5 T. lard
- 10 T. water
- ¼ t. salt

③
- 1 c. flour
- 5 T. lard or shortening

❶ Filling: Briefly heat the honey or maltose of ① until soft; remove from heat. Add honey, butter and flour in order to the sifted sugar (Fig. 1). Mix and knead into a smooth dough (Fig. 2). Remove, slightly flatten the dough and cut it into 20 pieces (Fig. 3).

❷ Skin: See p. 25, Turnip Cakes, step ❷.

❸ Lightly flatten each piece of skin and place a portion of filling in center of it. Gather edges of the skin to enclose filling; pinch to seal. Use a rolling pin to roll each filled piece into a 2-inch flat circle. Preheat oven to 350°; place the cakes on a cookie sheet and bake for 10 minutes; remove and cool. Serve.

餡：①
- 紅豆沙………（1斤）2杯
- 食用紅粉……………適量
- 水……………………適量
- 紗布或毛巾紙………1塊（20公分×20公分）

油酥皮：②
- 麵粉…………………2杯
- 猪油…………………5大匙
- 水……………………10大匙
- 塩……………………¼小匙

③
- 麵粉…………………1杯
- 猪油…………………5大匙

❶餡：豆沙分成20份，並揉成圓球狀備用。

❷油酥皮：參照第25頁「臘味蘿蔔餅」做法❷，做成油酥皮，共做20份。

❸將做好油酥皮，壓成直徑8公分之圓形麵皮，包入豆沙餡，並輕壓成直徑5公分之圓餅（圖4）。
將①料內之紗布浸水後再握乾。食用紅粉加水調勻，加在濕的紗布上，印花模型沾些顏色蓋在圓餅的光滑面上（圖5. 6.）。置烤盤上以350度烤20分鐘即成。

■豆沙做法參照第13頁。

■月餅模型本公司有售。

Short Moon Cakes　Makes 20

Filling:
①
- 2 c. red bean paste*
- food coloring
- water
- 1 sheet of paper towel or cloth (8″x8″)

Skin:
②
- 2 c. flour
- 5 T. lard
- 10 T. water
- ¼ t. salt

③
- 1 c. flour
- 5 T. lard

stamp (cookie design) of choice

❶ Filling: Divide the filling into 20 portions and shape them into balls.

❷ Skin: See p. 25, Turnip cake, step ❷

❸ Flatten each piece of dough lightly with the palm of the hand to form a 3-inch circle. Place 1 portion of filling in the center of the dough. Gather the edges to enclose the filling and pinch to seal. Flatten the dough to a 2-inch circle (Fig. 4). Dampen a sheet of paper towel. Mix food coloring with water then pour it on the towel. Take some food coloring on the stamp design then lightly press it on the dough (Figs. 5, 6). Make the remaining cakes in the same manner. Preheat oven to 350°. Place the cakes on a cookie sheet and bake for 20 minutes. Remove and serve.

* See p.13, "Sweet Buns with Red Bean Paste", for direction to prepare red bean paste.

■ Design stamp is available through Wei-Chuan's Cooking.

餡：
- 生鹹蛋黃‥‥‥‥‥20個
- 豆沙‥‥‥‥‥‥‥4杯
- 蛋黃‥‥‥‥‥‥‥1個
- 月餅模型‥‥‥‥‥1個

皮：
①
- 麵粉‥‥‥‥‥‥4½杯
- 奶粉‥‥‥‥‥‥½杯
- 發粉‥‥‥‥‥‥½大匙

②
- 糖‥‥‥‥‥‥1¼杯
- 蛋‥‥‥‥‥‥4個

奶油（溶化）‥‥‥‥¾杯

❶餡：鹹蛋黃盛烤盤內，以350°烤10分鐘。豆沙分成20份，把烤好的鹹蛋黃包入豆沙內並搓成圓球狀。

❷皮：將①料篩過。②料用打蛋器打10分鐘，隨入溶化的奶油及篩過的①料，輕輕翻拌成麵糰，分切成20小塊。

❸模型內撒入少許麵粉。將麵糰壓成直徑10公分圓形麵皮，包入豆沙球（餡），放入模型內壓緊（圖1.2.），印好花樣輕扣倒出（圖3），置烤盤上，表面塗蛋黃。將烤箱燒熱至400°F，放入中層烤30分鐘呈金黃色即成。

■亦可用其他餡來做，如蓮蓉、棗泥、白豆沙、五仁，如無鹹蛋黃可免用。

Cantonese-style Moon Cakes

Makes 20

Filling:
- 20 salty egg yolks
- 4 c. red bean paste
- 1 egg yolk
- 1 moon cake mold
- ¾ c. melted butter

Dough:
- ①
  - 4½ c. flour
  - ½ c. powdered milk
  - ½ T. baking powder
- ②
  - 1¼ c. sugar
  - 4 eggs

¾ c. melted butter

Filling: Preheat oven to 350°. Place the egg yolks on a cookie sheet and bake them for 10 minutes; remove. Divide the red bean paste into 20 portions. Put 1 egg yolk into 1 portion of the bean paste. Use the hands to roll it into a ball so that the bean paste covers the egg yolk.

Dough: Sift ①. Beat ② for 10 minutes. Add melted butter then add ①; lightly mix well. Divide the mixture into 20 portions.

Preheat the oven to 400°F. Take 1 portion of dough and flatten it with the palm of the hand to form a 4-inch circle. Place 1 portion of filling in the center of the dough and wrap it to enclose the filling. Pinch the edges to seal them. Roll the dough to form a ball and surface is smooth. Lightly flour the mold and place the filled dough in the mold (Fig. 1); press the dough to fill the mold (Fig. 2). Gently tap the mold to loosen the dough and to remove it (Fig. 3). Make the other cakes in the same manner. Place the cakes on a cookie sheet and brush egg yolk on top of them. Bake for 30 minutes; remove and serve.

Lotus nut paste, date paste and white bean paste may be substituted for red bean paste. Salty egg yolk may be omitted, if unavailable.

The moon cake mold may be purchased through Wei-Chuan's Cooking.

①
- 糖粉‥‥‥‥‥‥‥1杯
- 豬油或奶油‥‥‥‥½杯

②
- 水‥‥‥‥‥‥‥1大匙
- 發粉‥‥‥‥‥‥1小匙
- 小蘇打‥‥‥‥‥½小匙
（預先溶化）

③
- 蛋‥‥‥‥‥‥‥1個
- 杏仁精‥‥‥‥‥3小滴

麵粉‥‥‥‥‥‥‥‥2杯
杏仁片‥‥‥‥‥‥‥½杯
杏仁‥‥‥‥‥‥‥‥20粒

❶①料內的豬油先放在盆裏，用打蛋器攪拌1分鐘，再把糖分三次邊攪拌邊加入（每次約拌1分鐘），混合後再加②料及③料攪拌約2分鐘，加入杏仁片（圖4），隨入麵粉輕拌成麵糰（圖5）。

❷將麵糰先搓成長條再分切20小塊，切口朝上壓扁成圓餅狀，排在烤盤上，圓餅中央置半粒杏仁（或放杏仁片），並用手指輕按成凹狀（圖6）。烤箱先燒熱至350°F，將烤盤置上層烤15分鐘呈金黃色即可。

Chinese Almond Cookies

Makes 20

- ①
  - 1 c. powdered sugar
  - 1½ c. lard, shortening or butter
- ②
  - 1 T. water
  - 1 t. baking powder
  - ½ t. baking soda
  } mix
- ③
  - 1 egg
  - 3 drops almond extract
  - 2 c. flour
  - ½ c. almond slices
  - 20 whole almonds

❶ Preheat the oven to 350°F. Beat the lard of ingredients ① for 1 minute; add the sugar in thirds and beat for 1 minute after each addition. Add ② and ③; mix for 2 minutes. Add almond slices (Fig. 4) then add the flour and mix to form dough (Fig. 5).

❷ Roll the dough into a long baton-like roll then divide it into 20 balls. Flatten each piece of dough with the palm of the hand. Grease a cookie sheet; place the flattened dough two inches apart. Place a whole almond in the center of each dough. Press the almonds into the center of the dough (Fig. 6). Bake for 15 minutes or when the cookies are golden; remove and serve.

馬拉糕 1 份

① { 雞蛋····················5 個
    黃砂糖················1½ 杯

② { 濃縮奶水(一小罐)··········¾ 杯
    香草片(壓碎)·····1 粒或香精 5 滴
    猪油或奶油(溶化)··········½ 杯
    碱粉或碱水············1 小匙

③ { 麵粉····················2 杯
    發粉················1 大匙

蒸盤(27公分×30公分×6公分)···1 個
玻璃紙(36公分×39公分)··········1 張

❶先將①料盛於乾淨容器內,用打蛋器打到起泡且糖完全溶化約 5 分鐘(圖 1)再加入②料續打 1 分鐘(圖 2)成蛋液。

❷③料過篩放入打好的蛋液內(圖 3),攪拌均勻即為蛋糊。

❸將玻璃紙舖於容器內,倒入蛋糊,水開大火蒸 30 分鐘即成。

■如無碱粉可免用,但稍覺粘膩。

■此為廣東式蛋糕,通常在飲茶飯店可以買到。

Steamed Sponge Cake ("Ma-La-Gau")

① { 5   eggs
    1½ c. brown sugar

② { ¾   c. evaporated milk
    5   drops vanilla extract
    ½   c. melted shortening or butter   } combine
    1   t. baking soda

③ { 2   c. flour
    1   T. baking powder
    baking pan (10⅝"x12"x2⅜")
    1   sheet plastic wrap (14⅜"x15½")

❶ Beat ① until thick and cream colored, about 5 minutes (Fig. 1); add combined ingredients ② (Fig. 2) and beat for 1 minute.

❷ Sift ingredients of ③ (Fig. 3) and fold into egg mixture to make the batter.

❸ Line the baking pan with plastic wrap. Pour the batter into the lined pan and place it in a steamer. Steam for 30 minutes over high heat. Remove and allow to cool; slice and serve.

◀ Baking soda may be omitted; however, the cake will not rise as much and will be "doughy".

◀ This cake is Cantonese style. It is available at Chinese restaurants that serve snacks.

鹹蛋糕 1 份

炸紅葱頭···················4 大匙
瘦絞肉·····················4 兩

① { 醬油················2 大匙
    糖··················1 小匙

② { 蛋(半斤)··············5 個
    糖················1½ 杯

麵粉····················1½ 杯
蒸盤(27公分×30公分×6公分)···1 個
玻璃紙(36公分×39公分)··········1 張

❶油 1 大匙燒熱,將絞肉炒勻,隨加①料炒乾備用。

❷將②料用打蛋器打至起白泡且硬挺(約 10 分鐘),即可加入篩過麵粉,輕輕攪勻成麵糊。

❸將玻璃紙舖於容器內,倒入一半麵糊抹平(圖 4),以大火蒸約 8 分鐘取出,撒上一半的紅葱頭及肉末(圖 5),並將另一半麵糊倒入(圖 6)抹平,剩下的紅葱頭及肉末撒在上面回鍋續蒸 8 分鐘即成。

■此為台式蛋糕,特殊的是帶有鹹味,有鹹肉末散撒在蛋糕上。

Salty Egg Cake

    4   T. minced, fried shallots
    ⅓   lb. chopped pork, leanest
① { 2   T. soy sauce
    1   t. sugar
② { 5   large eggs
    1½ c. sugar
    1½ c. sifted flour
    1   sheet plastic wrap (14⅜"x15½")
    baking pan (10⅝"x12"x2⅜")

❶ Heat the wok then add 1 T. oil. Stir-fry chopped pork until color changes; add ① and stir-fry; remove.

❷ Beat ② until fairly stiff (at least 10 minutes); fold in the flour.

❸ Line the pan with plastic wrap; pour one half of the batter into the pan and spread it evenly (Fig. 4). Place the pan in a steamer and steam for 8 minutes. Remove and sprinkle with one half of the shallots and ground pork (Fig. 5). Pour the rest of the batter evenly over the steamed cake (Fig. 6). Sprinkle with the rest of the shallots and ground pork; return to steamer and steam for 8 minutes. Remove, slice, and serve.

■ This is Taiwanese Style cake. The salty taste and salty meat on top of the cake make this cake unique.

水　餃　50個

餡：絞肉‥‥‥‥‥‥‥12兩　　　塩‥‥‥‥‥‥‥‥1小匙
　　┌麻油‥‥‥‥‥‥6大匙　　韮菜或葱‥‥‥‥‥4兩
①│糖‥‥‥‥‥‥‥2小匙　　皮：②┌麵粉‥‥‥‥‥3杯
　│塩‥‥‥‥‥‥‥¾小匙　　　　　└冷水‥‥‥‥‥¾杯
　└胡椒‥‥‥‥‥‥¼小匙　　麵粉(備粘手時用)‥‥‥½杯
包心菜‥‥‥‥‥‥‥12兩

❶餡：絞肉加①料拌勻。包心菜剁碎加塩1小匙拌醃約
　　15分鐘後擠出水。韮菜切碎。將所有材料一起攪拌均
　　勻即爲餡。

❷皮：麵粉盛入盆內，加冷水拌合，再揉成麵糰，軟硬
　　要適中，取出放在板上繼續揉至十分光滑，擱置約10
　　分鐘醒麵，再搓成長條，切成50個小塊，分別趕成圓
　　薄片，即成餃子皮。

❸餡置皮中間，將皮捏合並將一邊推出一摺，再捏緊，
　　如此反覆至全部捏合即成餃子(圖1. 2. 3.)。

❹半鍋水燒開，放入餃子，用湯杓順著鍋邊推動以免粘
　　住，用大火煮開，再改小火煮6分鐘，即可撈出盛盤，
　　吃時沾醋、醬油、麻油、辣醬等。

■水餃皮如買市面上現成的，使用時需在封口處沾水。

■冷凍過的水餃煮時，先將水燒開再把冰凍的水餃放入，
　改小火煮10分鐘，煮時用湯杓輕輕推動，粘著的水餃
　便會散開。

Meat Dumplings ("Shwei Jaudz")
Makes 50

Filling:
1　lb.　ground pork (or beef)
┌6　T.　sesame oil
①│2　t.　sugar
　│¾　t.　salt
　└¼　t.　pepper
1　lb.　cabbage
1　t.　salt
⅓　lb.　chopped green onions
Skin:
②┌3　c.　flour
　└¾　c.　cold water
½　c.　flour (to prevent sticking during kneading)

❶ Filling: Mix ground pork and ① well. Chop cabbage
until fine. Mix the cabbage with 1 t. salt and let sit for 10
minutes; squeeze out the excess water. Mix the cabbage,
ground pork, and green onions well.

❷ Skin: In a bowl, add water to the flour and knead into a
smooth dough; let it stand for 10 minutes. Roll the dough
into a long baton-like roll and cut it into 50 pieces.
Use a rolling pin to roll each piece to a thin circle.

❸ Place 1 portion (¹⁄₅₀) of filling in the center of a dough
circle. Fold the circle in half and moisten the edges with
water. Use index finger and thumb to bring the sides
together (Fig. 1) to pleat one edge while keeping the
other edge smooth (Fig. 2). The smooth edge will give
conform to the decreased length of the pleated edge.
Pinch the pleats together then pinch them to seal
(Fig. 3). Repeat procedure for the other dumplings.

❹ Boil 10 cups of water and add dumplings; stir to prevent
dumplings from sticking together. Bring to a boil; turn the
heat to low and cook for 6 minutes. Remove. When
serving, use vinegar, soy sauce, sesame oil, hot bean
paste, etc. as a dipping sauce.
If using ready-made skins, seal the edges of the skins with
water.
To cook frozen dumplings: Bring water to a boil then add
the dumplings. Turn the heat to low and cook for
10 minutes; stir lightly to separate the dumplings.

鍋　貼　50個

餡：同「水餃」　　　　　　　油‥‥‥‥‥‥‥‥2大匙
皮：同「水餃」

❶餡：參照「水餃」做法❶。
❷皮：參照「水餃」做法❷。
❸參照「水餃」做法❸，將皮、餡包成水餃樣。
❹油燒熱，將餃子依序排在鍋內(圖4)，以小火煎約1
　分鐘呈金黃色時(圖5)，淋入水約半杯，並將鍋蓋蓋
　緊(圖6)用中火燜煮約6分鐘待水乾後即可鏟出。

■煎時使用不粘的平底鍋較理想。如爲冰凍過的水餃煎
　時需淋¾杯的水，燜煮時間亦需延長至10分鐘。

> 餃子餡內所使用的青菜可隨意選用，如大白菜、青
> 江菜、芹菜、紅蘿蔔等均可用。

Golden Fried Meat Dumplings
Makes 50

Filling: Same as filling for "Meat Dumplings"
Skin: Same as skin for "Meat Dumplings"
2　T.　oil

❶ Filling: See step ❶ of "Meat Dumplings"
❷ Skin: See step ❷ of "Meat Dumplings"
❸ See step ❸ of "Meat Dumplings".
❹ Heat the pan then add 2 T. oil. Arrange the dumplings,
flat side down, to line the pan (Fig. 4). Turn the heat
to low and fry the dumplings for 1 minute or until
golden brown (Fig. 5); add ½ cup hot water and cover
(Fig. 6). Cook for 6 minutes over medium heat or until
almost all water has evaporated; remove and serve
with soy sauce, sesame oil and vinegar.

■ A non-stick frying pan is preferred for frying dumplings.
If frozen meat dumplings are used, add ¾ cup water
instead of ½ cup and extend the cooking time from
6 to 10 minutes.

> Nappa cabbage, bok choy, celery, carrot, etc.
> may be used as a filling.

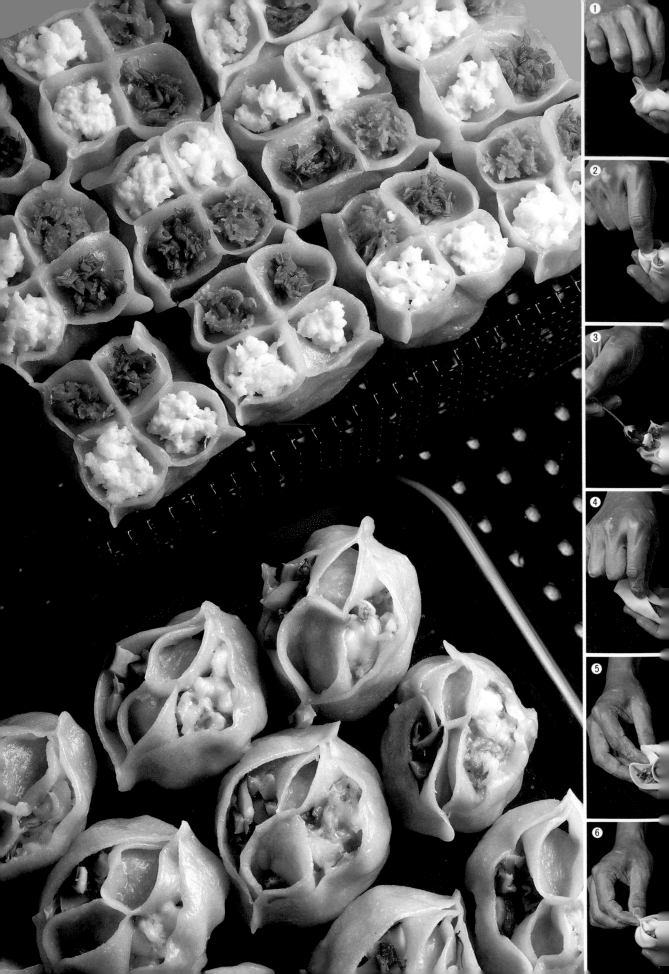

館：
①
蝦仁…………10兩
肥肉…………1兩
熟筍…………1杯
葱末、薑末…各1大匙

②
太白粉、料酒
…………各1大匙
麻油…………½大匙
糖…………2小匙
塩…………¾小匙
胡椒…………¼小匙

皮：麵粉…………2½杯

③
滾水…………½杯
冷水…………¼杯
猪油…………1大匙

④
葱…………少許
紅蘿蔔…………少許
蛋黃(炒半熟)…少許
蛋白(炒凝固)…少許
分別切碎

❶館：將①料內之蝦仁切粗粒，肥肉切碎，筍切小片（擠乾水份）。①料與②料一同拌勻即成「館」。

❷皮：麵粉2杯（另半杯黏手時用），先將③料之滾水冲入攪拌，再入冷水及猪油拌勻，揉成麵糰，分成24個小麵塊，用趕麵桿趕成直徑6公分之圓薄皮。

❸每張皮包上適量之館，由對角捏緊（圖1），留出四個孔（圖2），分別以④料裝飾（圖3）。入鍋以大火蒸約7分鐘即成。

"Four-flavor" Dumplings
Makes 24

Filling:
①
⅝ lb. raw, shelled shrimp
1½ oz. pork fat
1 c. precooked bamboo shoots
1 T. each: chopped green onions,
            chopped ginger root

②
1 T. each: cornstarch,
            cooking wine
½ t. sesame oil
2 t. sugar
¾ t. salt
¼ t. pepper

Skin:
③
2½ c. flour
½ c. boiling water
¼ c. cold water
1 lard or shortening

Garnish with:
④
green onions
carrot
egg yolk, stir-fry to half solid
egg white, stir fry to solid
} chopped

❶ Filling: Rinse and devein the shrimp; cut each shrimp into 3 sections. Dice the pork fat and cut the bamboo shoots into small, thinly sliced pieces. Squeeze the bamboo shoots to remove any liquid. Mix ① with ② thoroughly.

❷ Skin: Put 2 cups flour in a bowl. Save ½ cup flour to dust on hands when kneading. Add boiling water of ingredients ③ and mix. Add cold water and lard of ingredients ③ and knead into a smooth dough. Roll the dough into a baton-like roll then cut it into 24 pieces. Use a rolling pin to roll each piece of dough into a thin 2-inch circle. Repeat for other pieces of dough.

❸ Place 1 portion (¹⁄₂₄) of the filling in the center of a dough circle. Pinch together the opposite edges at the midpoint, bring the other opposite edges to the midpoint and squeeze together to form four loops (Fig. 1). Shape the loops, similar to a four-leaf clover (Fig. 2). Fill each section with one ingredient of ④ (Fig. 3). Follow the same procedure for the other pieces of dough. Steam the dumpling over boiling water, over high heat for 7 minutes; remove and serve.

館：
①
絞肉…………½斤
荸薺…………6個
紅蘿蔔…………⅓條
蝦仁…………2兩
葱、薑末…各1大匙

②料同「四方餃」

皮：麵粉…………2½杯

③料同「四方餃」

④
蝦仁…………少許
香菇…………少許
分別切碎

❶館：將①料剁碎。絞肉與①、②料一同拌勻成「館」。

❷皮：參照「四方餃」做法❷。

❸每張皮包上適量之館，捏成鳳眼形狀（圖4.5.6.），將兩眼內以④料裝飾。入鍋以大火蒸7分鐘即成。

"Phoenix-eye" Dumplings
Makes 24

Filling:
①
⅔ lb. ground meat, pork or beef
6 water chestnuts
⅓ carrot, 3 inches long
3 oz. raw, shelled shrimp
1 T. each: green onions,
            chopped ginger root
② Use the same ingredients as ② of "Four-flavor" Dumplings

Skin:
2½ c. flour
③ Use the same ingredients as ③ of "Four-flavor" Dumplings

Garnish with:
④
raw, shelled shrimp
presoftened Chinese Black mushrooms
} chopped

❶ Filling: finely chop ①. In a bowl, mix the ground pork, ①, and ② thoroughly.

❷ Skin: Follow the step ❷ of "Four-flavor" Dumplings.

❸ Place 1 portion (¹⁄₂₄) of filling in the center of a dough circle; pinch together the opposite edges at midpoint (Fig. 4). Fold in half at open ends (Fig. 5). Press the ends together to form a crescent-shape and resembles the eyes of a phoenix (Fig. 6). Sprinkle both ovals with ④. Follow the same procedure for the other pieces of dough. Steam the dumplings over boiling water, over high heat for 7 minutes; remove and serve.

餡：蝦仁……………………½斤　　皮：　澄麵…………1 ½杯
　　┌料酒…………1 大匙　　② ┤滾水…………1 杯
　　│太白粉………½大匙　　　　└猪油…………1 大匙
① ┤糖、麻油……各1 小匙
　　│塩……………¾小匙
　　└胡椒…………¼小匙
熟肥肉(切小片)………2 兩
熟筍(切小片)…………3 兩

❶餡：蝦仁切粗粒，加①料拌匀，再拌入肥肉及筍即成「餡」。

❷皮：將②料攪匀，揉成麵糰，分切成30個小麵塊。刀面抹油壓成圓薄皮(圖1. 2.)(或用趕麵桿來做)。

❸每張皮包上適量之餡，包成餃子狀(圖3. 4. 5.)。入鍋以大火蒸約5 分鐘即成。

■注意：皮的厚薄若做的不匀或太薄，蒸熟後易破裂，若蒸的時間過長也會發生破裂現象。

Steamed Shrimp Dumplings I
Makes 30

Filling:
⅔ lb. raw, shelled shrimp
① ┌ 1 T. cooking wine
　 │ ½ T. cornstarch
　 ┤ 1 t. sugar, sesame oil
　 │ ¾ t. salt
　 └ ¼ t. pepper
3 oz. pork fat, diced finely
4 oz. precooked bamboo shoots
Skin:
② ┌ 1½ c. non-glutinous flour(澄麵)
　 ┤ 1 c. boiling water
　 └ 1 T. lard or shortening

❶ Filling: Rinse and devein the shrimp; drain and dice them coarsely. In a bowl, mix the shrimp with ① then add the pork fat and bamboo shoots.

❷ Skin: Mix Ingredients ② together and knead it into a smooth dough; divide the dough into 30 pieces. Grease a cleaver with oil then use the flat side of the cleaver to press each piece of dough into a thin circle (Figs. 1, 2). A rolling pin may be used to shape the dough circle.

❸ Place 1 portion of the filling (1/30) in the center of a dough circle. Hold the filled circle with one hand and fold it slightly. Starting at the end, use the index finger and thumb of the other hand to pinch the ends of the same side together (Fig. 3). Gather the outside edge to form pleats (Fig. 4). Pinch the edges together (Fig. 5). Follow the same procedure for the other pieces of dough. Steam the filled dumpling over high heat for 5 minutes; remove and serve.

◀ The dough should be evenly stretched to prevent it from breaking during steaming. The dough may also break if it is too thin or steamed too long.

餡：蝦仁……………………½斤
　　①料同「蝦餃」
　　筍或荸薺(切小片)………½杯
　　香菇末、香菜末……各¼杯
皮：②料同「蝦餃」

❶餡：蝦仁切粗粒，與①料、筍、香菇、香菜末一同拌匀成「餡」。

❷皮：參照「蝦餃」做法❷。

❸每張皮包上適量之餡，將皮對折捏緊成餃子狀(圖6)。入鍋以大火蒸5 分鐘即成。

Steamed Shrimp Dumplings II
Makes 30

Filling:
⅔ lb. raw, shelled shrimp
① Use the same ingredients as ① of Steamed Shrimp Dumplings I
½ c. bamboo shoots or water chestnuts, cut into small slices
¼ c. each: pre-softened Chinese black mushrooms, coriander } chopped
Skin: Use the same ingredients as ② of Steamed Shrimp Dumplings I

❶ Filling: Devein and rinse the shrimp; drain and dice it coarsely. Mix the shrimp with ①, bamboo shoots, Chinese black mushrooms, and coriander.

❷ Skin: Follow step ❷ of Steamed Shrimp Dumplings I.

❸ Put 1 portion of the filling (1/30) in the center of a dough circle. Hold the filled circle with one hand and fold it slightly. Starting at one end, use the index finger and thumb of the other hand to pinch the opposite edges together (Fig. 6). Follow the same step for the other pieces of dough. Steam the dumpling over high heat for 5 minutes; remove and serve.

餡
- 里肌肉⋯⋯⋯⋯⋯10兩
- 肥肉⋯⋯⋯⋯⋯1兩
- 香菇⋯⋯⋯⋯⋯4朵
- 熟筍⋯⋯⋯⋯⋯1枝

①
- 太白粉⋯⋯⋯1½大匙
- 料酒⋯⋯⋯⋯1大匙
- 麻油⋯⋯⋯⋯½大匙
- 糖⋯⋯⋯⋯⋯1小匙
- 塩⋯⋯⋯⋯⋯¾小匙
- 胡椒⋯⋯⋯⋯¼小匙

皮：餛飩皮⋯⋯⋯⋯24張
青豆仁⋯⋯⋯⋯⋯24粒

❶餡：里肌肉、肥肉、香菇均切小丁，筍切小片，加①料順同一方向用力攪勻，並甩打約3〜4分鐘成餡。

❷餛飩皮修圓（圖1），將餡置當中（圖2），用手捏起，中間放一粒青豆仁，用匙沾水在餡上抹平（圖3），全部做好，入鍋大火蒸約6分鐘即成。

Pork Shau Mai　Makes 24

Filling:
- ¾ lb. pork loin
- 1⅓ oz. pork fat
- 4 pre-softened Chinese black mushrooms
- 1 precooked bamboo shoot

①
- 1⅛ T. cornstarch
- 1 T. cooking wine
- ½ T. sesame oil
- 1 t. sugar
- ¾ t. salt
- ¼ t. pepper

Skin: 30 won ton skins
24 green peas

❶ Filling: Dice the pork loin, pork fat, black mushrooms, and bamboo shoot. Place in a mixing bowl. Add ① and stir in the same direction until mixed well. Throw mixture against the inside of the bowl for 3-4 minutes so that the ingredients combine thoroughly; divide into 24 portions.

❷ Trim the won ton skins to make them round (Fig. 1). Place 1 portion of filling in the center of a won ton skin (Fig. 2). Take the won ton skin between the index finger and thumb, gather edges together to make a waist. Place 1 green pea in the center of the filling; use a knife, dipped in water, to press down the filling so that it is smooth and compact (Fig. 3). Follow step ❷ for the remaining dough and filling. Place the finished shau mai in a steamer about ½-inch apart. Steam for 6 minutes over high heat; remove. Serve.

牛絞肉⋯⋯⋯⋯⋯⋯⋯12兩

①
- ①料同「豬肉燒賣」
- 香菜末⋯⋯⋯⋯2大匙
- 陳皮末⋯⋯⋯⋯1大匙

青菜葉⋯⋯⋯⋯⋯24片

❶牛絞肉加①料，仔細拌勻至肉的黏性很大後再醃10分鐘（圖4）即為餡。

❷將餡用手搓成大丸子（圖5），用湯匙沾水把丸子一個個捥出來（圖6）並墊上青菜葉，共做24個丸子，排入蒸盤內，水開大火蒸8分鐘至熟即可。

Beef Shau Mai　Makes 24

- 1 lb. ground beef

①
- ① Use the same ingredients as ① of "Pork Shau Mai"
- 2 T. chopped coriander
- 1 T. chopped orange peel

24 cabbage, lettuce, or similar leaves

❶ Filling: Mix ground beef and ① thoroughly until the meat is sticky (Fig. 4) then marinate it for 10 minutes.

❷ Squeeze 1 portion of the filling (¹⁄₂₄) into a ball (Fig. 5). Dip a spoon in water then use the spoon to remove the meatball (Fig. 6). Place the meatball on a leaf. Follow step ❷ for the remaining filling. Arrange the meatballs in a steamer and steam over high heat for 8 minutes.

糯米燒賣 32個

餡：糯米……………1½杯

①
- 肉丁……………1杯
- 香菇、蝦米丁……各¼杯

②
- 醬油……………2大匙
- 料酒……………½大匙
- 糖……………1小匙
- 塩……………½小匙
- 胡椒……………¼小匙

皮：餛飩皮……………32張

③
- 葱花(取綠莖)……2大匙
- 蛋皮(切碎)………2大匙

❶餡：糯米洗淨，加水1¼杯浸泡半小時。煮開1分鐘後改小火續煮20分鐘，熄火，再燜10分鐘。或用電鍋煮成糯米飯，再用筷子撥散。
油2大匙燒熱，先炒香①料，再加②料並拌入糯米飯即成「餡」。

❷餛飩皮修圓，每張皮放上一份餡，包成燒賣（圖1. 2. 3），撒上適量③料。水開大火蒸4分鐘即成。

Sweet Rice Shau Mai

Makes 32

Filling:
1½ c. sweet rice

①
- 1 c. diced pork or beef
- ¼ c. each: Chinese black mushroom, diced dried shrimp

②
- 2 T. soy sauce
- ½ T. Cooking wine
- 1 t. sugar
- ½ t. salt
- ¼ t. pepper

Skin: 32 won ton skins

③
- 2 T. chopped green onions, green part only
- 2 T. diced egg sheet

❶ Filling: Clean rice then soak it in 1¼ cups water for 30 minutes. Bring the water to a boil for 1 minute; turn the heat to low and continue to cook for 20 minutes. Turn off the heat and simmer the rice for 10 minutes. OR use a rice cooker to cook the rice.
Heat the wok then add 2 T. oil. Stir-fry ① until fragrant; add ② and the rice; stir until mixed well.

❷ Trim the won ton skins to make them round. Place 1 portion of filling (1/32) in the center of a won ton skin. Bring the opposite edges together and pinch them together to hold (Fig. 1). Shape loops, similar to a four-leaf clover (Fig. 2). Fill the loops with ③ (Fig. 3). Follow step ❷ for the other shau mai. Place the finished shou mai in a steamer about ½-inch apart. Steam over high heat for 4 minutes; remove and serve.

魚翅餃 32個

餡：

①
- 蝦仁、里肌肉……各6兩
- 魚翅……………3兩
- 香菜或青葱…………½杯
- 肥肉或豬油………2大匙

②
- 太白粉、麻油…各½大匙
- 糖……………2小匙
- 塩……………1小匙
- 胡椒……………¼小匙

皮：餛飩皮……………32張

❶餡：將①料均切小丁，調入②料用力攪拌至有黏性，即成「餡」。

❷餛飩皮修圓，每張皮包入一份餡，包成如餃子形（圖4. 5. 6.）。水開用大火蒸約6分鐘即可供食。

■市面上賣的魚翅餃，皮多呈黃色，是加入雞蛋做的。

Shark's Fin Dumplings

Makes 32

Filling:

①
- ½ lb. raw, shelled shrimp
- ½ lb. pork loin
- ¼ lb. pre-softened shark's fin*
- ½ c. green vegetable or green onions
- 2 T. pork fat or lard

②
- ½ T. each: cornstarch, sesame oil
- 2 t. sugar
- 1 t. salt
- ¼ t. pepper

Skin: 32 won ton skins

❶ Filling: Dice ingredients in ①; place in a bowl and add ②. Mix thoroughly to combine ingredients.

❷ Trim won ton skins to make them round. Place a portion of filling (1/32) in the center of a won ton skin; fold in half. Use index finger and thumb to bring opposite edges together (Fig. 4). Gathering edge of skin to form pleates (Fig. 5). Pinch ends to seal (Fig. 6). Follow step ❷ for the reamining filling. Place finished dumplings in a steamer and steam over high heat for 6 minutes; remove and serve.

* To soften dried shark's fin, place in water to cover and heat until just boiling; turn off heat and allow to soak until water is cool. Remove and scrub the fin lightly to remove any filmy covering. Soak in water overnight. Repeat procedure 3-4 times, changing the water each time, until shark's fin is very soft. Use as directed.

■ Shark's Fin Dumplings, with egg won ton skins, are available in markets. To make egg won ton skins, an egg is added to the dough.

鮮蝦燒賣　24個

餡：蝦仁‥‥‥‥‥‥‥‥8兩　　皮：餛飩皮‥‥‥‥‥‥48張
　　　　　　　　　　　　　　中蝦(去殼留尾)‥‥‥‥24條
　　┌料酒、麻油‥‥‥各½大匙
　　│太白粉‥‥‥‥‥‥2小匙
①　│糖‥‥‥‥‥‥‥‥1小匙
　　│塩‥‥‥‥‥‥‥‥½小匙
　　└胡椒‥‥‥‥‥‥‥¼小匙
　　┌荸薺(切碎)‥‥‥‥½杯
②　│香菜‥‥‥‥‥‥‥3大匙
　　└絞肥肉或豬油‥‥‥2大匙

❶蝦仁切粗粒，加入①料拌勻，隨入②料再攪勻即為「餡」。

❷每張皮放上1份餡(圖1)，上加一條蝦(圖2)，再蓋上一張皮包緊(圖3)，共做24個，水開大火蒸8分鐘即成。

Shrimp Shau Mai　*Makes 24*

Filling:
½　lb. raw, shelled shrimp
　　┌½　T. each: cooking wine, sesame oil
　　│2　t.　cornstarch
①　│1　t.　sugar
　　│½　t.　salt
　　└¼　t.　pepper
　　┌½　c. chopped chestnuts
②　│3　T.　coriander
　　└2　T.　ground pork fat or lard
Skin: 48 won ton skins
24 raw, shelled medium shrimp, with tail intact

❶　Filling: Chop shrimp coarsely then mix it with ①; add ② and mix thoroughly.

❷　Put 1 portion of the filling on a skin (Fig. 1). Place a shrimp on top of the filling (Fig. 2); cover the shrimp with another skin and let the tail stick out between the two skins. Wrap the two skins around the filling (Fig. 3). Follow step ❷ for the remaining filling. Place the finished shau mai in a steamer about ½-inch apart. Steam for 8 minutes over high heat; remove and serve.

鵪蛋燒賣　20個

　　┌里肌肉‥‥‥‥‥‥4兩　　鵪蛋‥‥‥‥‥‥‥‥20個
餡　│蝦仁‥‥‥‥‥‥‥2兩　　皮：餛飩皮‥‥‥‥‥20張
　　│肥肉或豬油‥‥‥1½大匙
　　└熟筍‥‥‥‥‥‥‥半枝
　　┌料酒、麻油‥‥‥各½大匙
　　│太白粉‥‥‥‥‥‥2小匙
①　│糖‥‥‥‥‥‥‥‥1小匙
　　│塩‥‥‥‥‥‥‥‥½小匙
　　└胡椒‥‥‥‥‥‥‥¼小匙

❶餡：里肌肉、蝦仁、肥肉均切小丁，筍切小片，加①料順同一方向用力拌合，並甩打約3～4分鐘成餡。鵪蛋煮熟去殼備用。

❷餛飩皮修圓，每張皮先放一個鵪蛋(圖4)，上置1份肉餡(圖5)用手捏起，用匙沾水在餡上抹平，翻過來(圖6)，共做20個。水開大火蒸6分鐘即成。

Quail Eggs Shau Mai　*Makes 20*

Filling:
　　┌⅓　lb pork loin
　　│⅙　lb raw, shelled shrimp
　　│1½　T.　pork fat or lard
　　└½　precooked bamboo shoot
　　┌½　T. each: cooking wine, sesame oil
　　│2　t.　cornstarch
①　│1　t.　sugar
　　│½　t.　salt
　　└¼　t.　pepper
20 quail eggs
Skin: 20 won ton skins

❶　Filling: Dice the pork loin, shrimp, pork fat, and bamboo shoot. Place in a mixing bowl and add ①; mix well. Throw the mixture against the inside of the bowl for 3-4 minutes so that ingredients combine thoroughly. Divide the mixture into 30 equal portions. Cook the quail eggs in boiling water until hard (about 5 minutes); remove and drain. Remove shell.

❷　Trim won ton skins to make them round; place a quail egg in the center of a won ton skin (Fig. 4); put 1 portion of filling on top of the egg (Fig. 5). Take the won ton skin between the index finger and thumb; gather edges together to make a waist. Use a spoon, dipped in water, to press down the filling so that it is smooth and compact. Follow step ❷ for the remaining filling. Place the finished shau mai, open side down (Fig. 6), in a steamer about ½-inch apart. Steam for 6 minutes over high heat; remove and serve.

炸餛飩

● 將包好的餛飩放入燒熱的「炸油」內，用中火炸約1分半鐘，呈金黃色即成。

■餛飩做法：參照「蝦仁餛飩」「豬肉餛飩」

蝦仁餛飩

24個

餡：蝦仁……………………4兩

① 太白粉、料酒…各1小匙
　 塩……………………¼小匙

熟筍(切小片)…………2大匙

薑末……………………1小匙

皮：餛飩皮………………24張

② 高湯或水……………6杯
　 塩……………………1¼小匙
　 料酒…………………1小匙

豆苗或其他青菜…………4兩

③（一人份）
　 葱末…………1大匙
　 醬油…………½大匙
　 麻油…………½小匙
　 胡椒…………¼小匙

❶蝦仁切粗粒，加①料及筍片、薑末拌勻成「餡」。每張餛飩皮包上適量的餡，即成餛飩。

❷將②料燒開，分別倒入備好③料之一人份湯碗內。

❸將餛飩及豆苗分別煮熟，放入做好的湯汁內即成。

■餛飩包法(一)：將餡放在皮中間，折成三角形(圖1)由1公分處向前折起(圖2)，兩端沾水粘住(圖3)。

Fried Won Tons

- Deep-fry the won tons over medium heat for 1½ minutes until golden.
- ■ For directions to make won tons see "Shrimp Won Ton Soup and "Pork Won Ton Soup".

Shrimp Won Ton Soup

Makes 24

Filling:
⅓ lb. raw, shelled shrimp
① (mix)
　1 t. each: cornstarch, cooking wine
　¼ t. salt
2 T. precooked bamboo shoots, diced
1 t. ground ginger root
Skin: 24 won ton skins
②
　6 c. stock or water
　1¼ t. salt
　1 t. cooking wine
5 oz. spinach or other leafy green vegetable
③ (for each serving)
　1 T. chopped green onions
　½ T. soy sauce
　½ t. sesame oil
　¼ t. pepper
3 bowls for 3 servings (8 won tons in each bowl)

❶ Devein and rinse shrimp; drain and dice them coarsely. In a bowl, mix the shrimp with ①, bamboo shoots, and ginger root to make the filling. Place 1 portion of the filling (1/24) in the center of a skin. See wrapping directions below to fold won tons. Wrap the won tons.

❷ Place ingredients ③ in each serving bowl; bring ② to a boil then portion it into each bowl.

❸ Boil the water in a pan then gently drop some won tons and spinach in the water; cook for 1 minute. Remove the won tons and drain then place the won tons and spinach into the serving bowls; serve.

■ Method I of wrapping a won ton: Diagonally fold the skin in half to form a triangle (Fig. 1). Fold the edge containing the filling over about ½ inch (Fig. 2). Bring the two points together; moisten one inner edge overlaps and pinch the ends together to hold (Fig. 3).

豬肉餛飩

24個

餡：絞肉……………………4兩

① 太白粉、麻油、料酒………
　 ……………………各1小匙
　 塩……………………⅓小匙
　 胡椒…………………少許

葱末……………………2大匙

皮：餛飩皮………………24張

② 高湯或水……………6杯
　 塩……………………1½小匙
　 料酒、麻油……各1小匙
　 胡椒…………………¼小匙

小白菜(切段)…………4兩

葱花……………………2大匙

❶絞肉加①料及葱末拌勻成「餡」。每張餛飩皮包上適量的餡，即成餛飩。

❷②料燒開，加入餛飩及小白菜再燒開，撒上葱花即成。

■餛飩如果份量少，可用此法燒煮簡單易做。若餛飩份量多，則需將湯與餛飩分開煮，否則煮出的湯較混。

■餛飩包法(二)：將餡放在皮中央(圖4)，把皮折起(圖5)姆指與食指捏緊，抽出小匙(圖6)再略捏緊即成。

Pork Won Ton Soup

Makes 24

Filling:
⅓ lb. ground pork
① (mix)
　1 t. each: cornstarch, sesame oil
　⅓ t. salt
　dash of pepper
2 T. chopped green onions
Skin: 24 won ton skins
②
　6 c. stock or water
　1½ t. salt
　1 t. each: cooking wine, sesame oil
　¼ t. pepper
⅓ lb. bok choy or other leafy green vegetable, cut into pieces
2 T. chopped green onions, green part

❶ In a bowl, mix ground pork, ①, and the chopped green onions thoroughly to make the filling. Put one portion of the filling (1/24) in the center of each skin; fold the skin to enclose filling.

❷ Bring ② to a boil then add the won tons and bok choy; bring to a boil again. Sprinkle the soup with chopped green onions.

■ If too many won tons are cooked in the soup, the soup will not be clear. This method of preparing won ton soup is best for fewer than 4 servings.

■ Method II of wrapping a won ton: Use a spoon to put filling in the center of the skin (Fig. 4); fold the corner of the skin over the meat-filled spoon and lightly pinch the skin with thumb and index finger to seal (Fig. 5). Remove the spoon and pinch the skin tightly (Fig. 6).

潤餅 16捲

餡：里肌肉絲……½杯
① 太白粉、料酒…各1小匙
　 塩……⅓小匙
② 綠豆芽……2杯
　 熟筍絲、五香豆干(切絲)……各1杯
　 熟紅蘿蔔絲……½杯
③ 糖……½大匙
　 塩、麻油……各1小匙
　 胡椒……¼小匙

皮：春捲皮……16張
香菜(略切)……1杯
花生粉……½杯
海鮮醬……¼杯

❶餡：里肌肉絲加①料拌匀。油4大匙燒熱，先炒里肌肉，再放入②料，並加③料炒匀成餡，盛盤備用。

❷每張春捲皮，一半邊緣塗少許海鮮醬(圖1)，中央放適量的餡及香菜、花生粉(圖2)包成長12公分的圓筒狀即成(圖3)。

■本省的習俗在尾牙(農曆12月16日)或清明節，家家戶戶都做潤餅捲過節。習慣上，將所有材料分別炒熟盛盤，也可二或三樣混合炒熟或部份青菜生吃，不止上項材料，可選蝦米、蒜白、黃瓜、唐好菜、包心菜、洋蔥、乾海藻、魷魚、蘿蔔乾等，依個人喜歡包捲著來吃。

■喜食甜味者可在花生粉內加4大匙細糖混合。

Taiwanese Egg Rolls

Makes 16

½ c. shredded pork loin
① 1 t. each: cornstarch, cooking wine } mix
　 ⅓ t. salt
② 2 c. bean sprouts
　 1 c. each: precooked bamboo shoot, pressed bean curd } shredded
　 ½ c. shredded, precooked carrot
③ ½ T. sugar
　 1 t. each: salt, sesame oil
　 ¼ t. pepper
Skin: 16 egg roll skins
1 c. coriander, chopped coarsely
½ c. crushed peanuts
¼ c. hoisin sauce

❶ Filling: Mix the pork with ①. Heat the pan then add 4 T. oil; stir-fry the pork, ②, and ③ until mixed well. Remove.

❷ Spread some hoisin sauce along one edge of a skin (Fig. 1). Place 1 portion ($\frac{1}{16}$) each: filling, coriander, and crushed peanuts in the center of the skin (Fig. 2). Fold the skin, without hoisin sauce, over the filling; roll the skin over again, tuck in the ends to form a 5-inch long roll (Fig. 3). Finish wrapping by folding the edge with hoisin sauce to seal the egg roll. Make the remaining rolls in the same manner.

■ Taiwanese egg rolls are served at year-end dinners given for employees by shop owners on the 16th day of the twelfth moon or served at Tomb-sweeping Day to commemorate an ancester. The various vegetables listed may be stir-fried in groups of 2 or 3 or served fresh. Lettuce, dried shrimp, long garlic stalks, cucumber, green beans, celery, seaweed, squid, or dried tunip may substitute ingredients in ② according to taste.

■ 4 T. sugar may be added to the crushed peanuts if a sweet taste is preferred.

炸春捲 16捲

餡：里肌肉絲……½杯
① 太白粉、料酒…各1小匙
　 塩……⅓小匙
綠豆芽、韮黃……各2杯(切2公分長)
紅蘿蔔絲……½杯
② 糖……1大匙
　 麻油……½大匙
　 塩……¾小匙
　 胡椒……¼小匙

皮：春捲皮……16張
麵糊：麵粉、水……各2大匙
「炸油」……適量

❶餡：里肌肉加①料拌匀，入油鍋炒熟盛出備用。綠豆芽、韮黃、紅蘿蔔以開水汆燙(10秒)立即撈起，瀝乾水份，與里肌肉絲、②料一同拌匀成餡，分成16份。

❷每張春捲皮前半部邊緣沾麵糊，中間放上一份餡(圖4)，包成長12公分圓筒狀(圖5. 6.)。

❸「炸油」燒熱，中火將春捲炸4分鐘至皮脆呈金黃色撈起盛盤。食用時沾上醬油或番茄醬、黑醋等。

■除綠豆芽、韮黃、紅蘿蔔材料外，也可用筍、包心菜四季豆、小黃瓜、芹菜等來做。

Fried Egg Rolls

Makes 16

Filling:
⅓ c. shredded pork loin
① 1 t. each: cornstarch, cooking wine
　 ⅓ t. salt
2 c. each: bean sprout; Chinese chives, cut to 1-inch sections
½ c. shredded carrot
② 1 T. sugar
　 ½ T. sesame oil
　 ¾ t. salt
　 ¼ t. pepper
Skin: 16 egg roll skins
Flour paste:
2 T. each: flour, water (mix)
oil

❶ Filling: In a bowl, mix the pork with ① well. Heat the pan then add 4 T. oil; stir-fry the pork until it changes color. Remove. Blanch the bean sprouts, carrots, and Chinese chives in boiling water for 10 seconds. Remove them and plunge them into cold water to cool; drain. In a bowl, mix the pork, carrots, bean sprouts, Chinese chives, and ② throughly. Divide the filling into 16 portions.

❷ Dab some flour paste along one corner of the top half of the skin. Place a portion of filling in the center of the skin (Fig. 4). Fold the lower third of the skin over the filling to one-third from the top corner. Fold in the two ends (Fig. 5). Continue to wrap the skin to form a baton-like roll (Fig. 6). Rolls should be about 4-inch long. Follow the same procedure for the other skins.

❸ Heat the oil and deep-fry the egg rolls over medium heat for 4 minutes or until they are golden brown; remove and drain. Serve with soy sauce, ketchup or vinegar.

■ Bamboo shoots, cabbage, string beans, cucumber or celery may be substituted for the bean sprout, Chinese chives and carrot.

春捲皮

中筋或高筋麵粉…………6杯
塩………………1½小匙
清水………………3杯

❶塩放入清水內待溶化,加入篩過麵粉拌勻,並以清水¼杯濕潤表面,以免乾燥,擱置半小時醒麵,至表面起泡。

❷用手將麵逐次自四週拉起向中央揉和,反覆數次至麵生筋。

❸以中火將平底鍋均勻燒熱,擦淨,並以油布將欲做春捲皮之大小周圍擦出一道圓形。

❹用手抓起一團麵(圖1)迅速自鐵鍋中央向外均勻地擦一圓形(圖2)隨將多餘之麵糰抓起,並將留在麵皮上的小麵粒按平,把麵皮略烙熟,皮邊稍有翻起現象時掀起即成春捲皮(圖3)。

■做春捲皮有專用之鐵板,如無可用厚的大平底鍋來做。若鍋過熱時,擦出之春捲皮會粘着手中之麵糰時,應以乾淨濕布擦拭鐵板,使熱度降低。

Egg Roll Skins   Makes 24

6 c. high protein flour, sifted
1½ t. salt
3 c. water

❶ Put the water and salt in a bowl; allow the salt to dissolve. Add the flour and mix until the batter is thick and smooth. Pour ¼ cup water on top of the batter to keep it from drying; let it stand for 30 minutes or until bubbles form on the surface.

❷ Use hands to pick up some batter from the edge of the bowl and drop it into the center of the batter. Continue to take batter from the edges and drop it in the center until all batter from the edges has been dropped into the center; repeat this process until the dough is smooth and elastic. Sprinkle a little water on top of the dough to keep it moist.

❸ Evenly heat a heavy grill over medium. Clean the grill; use an oil-soaked cloth to oil a 6-inch round surface on the grill.

❹ Take a handful of batter (Fig. 1) and lightly "wipe" the grill with it in a circular motion (Fig. 2) to make a 6-inch thin pancake. Remove the excess batter immediately. Lightly pop any bubbles on the skin. When the edges of the skin begin to curl, peel off the skin (Fig. 3) and place it on a serving plate. Repeat step ❹ to make more skins.

■ The skins will stick to the grill if it is too hot; to cool the grill, lightly wipe it with a moistened cloth. Oil the grill again with the oil-soaked cloth.

薩其馬   1份

① { 麵粉…………1½杯
發粉…………¾大匙 }

蛋(大)…………2個
水…………2大匙
「炸油」…………適量

② { 糖…………½杯
麥芽糖或蜂蜜…………⅓杯
水…………⅙杯
檸檬汁或醋…………½大匙 }

鋁盤(27公分×30公分×6公分)…………1個

③ { 炒熟白芝麻…………½大匙
葡萄乾…………2大匙
香菜、紅綠絲…各2大匙
花生粉…………½杯 }

❶蛋加水2大匙打散,放入過篩之①料內拌合,並揉成軟硬適中之麵糰(黏手時撒上乾麵粉)放置30分鐘醒麵。

❷將麵糰趕成厚0.2公分之大方形薄片,再切成3公分寬之麵片,繼而切成細條。

❸「炸油」燒熱,中火將麵條炸呈淡黃色撈出盛於鍋內。

❹將②料以中火燒開後改小火熬煮2分鐘至糖完全溶化成蜜狀濃度時(圖4),即可淋在炸過之麵條上(圖5)迅速拌勻。③料置鋁盤內,將麵條倒入(圖6)壓成厚四公分四方大塊,待冷切塊即成。

■③料內之佐料可任選數種方便購買的或個人喜愛的即可。

"Sa-Ji-Ma"

① { 1½ c. flour
¾ T. baking powder } sifted

2 large eggs
2 t. water
oil

② { ½ c. sugar
⅙ c. maltose or honey
⅙ c. water
½ T. lemon juice or vinegar }

baking pan (11"x12"x2")

③ { ½ T. pre-cooked white sesame seeds
2 T. raisins
2 T. each: coriander,
            shredded red or green candied fruit
½ c. crushed peanuts }

❶ In a bowl, beat the eggs and 2 T. water. Add ① and knead it into a smooth dough; add flour, if the dough is too sticky. Let the dough stand for 30 minutes.

❷ Roll out the dough. Cut the dough into 1-inch strips then shred them in the opposite direction to ¼" pieces.

❸ Heat the oil for deep-frying; add the shreds and deep-fry them over medium heat until light golden. Remove and drain. Place the shreds in a large mixing bowl.

❹ Bring ② to a boil; turn the heat to low and cook for 2 minutes or until the sugar is completely dissolved (Fig. 4). Pour the mixture over the fried shreds (Fig. 5); immediately mix well to coat them. Place ③ in the baking pan. Spread the coated shreds in the pan (Fig. 6) and press them to a compact, 1½" thick; allow the cake to cool and cut it into pieces. Serve.

■ Ingredients ③ may be changed according to taste.

麵粉‥‥‥‥‥‥‥‥‥‥‥‥ 1½杯
①{ 水‥‥‥‥‥‥‥‥‥‥‥‥ 1杯
　 塩‥‥‥‥‥‥‥‥‥‥‥‥ ⅛小匙
蛋（大3個）‥‥‥‥‥‥‥‥‥ 1杯
細砂糖‥‥‥‥‥‥‥‥‥‥‥ 4大匙
「炸油」‥‥‥‥‥‥‥‥‥‥‥ 適量

❶麵粉篩過兩次置容器内。蛋打散。
❷①料燒開，冲入麵粉内，攪拌，再將蛋液分次加入與麵糰混合均匀。
❸「炸油」用小火略燒熱。抓起麵糰擠成丸子，用湯匙沾油把麵丸一個個挽出，隨即放入油鍋内（圖1.2.），俟全部做完後改中火炸，臨起鍋前再改大火，前後炸7分鐘至脹大約3倍呈金黄色（圖3）撈起，滾上細砂糖即成。
■「炸油」最好用乾淨油，炸出來顏色才好看。做好的白糖沙翁可依個人喜愛鑲入各種口味的果醬。

Sugar-coated Puffs Makes 16

1½　c.　flour
① { 1　c.　water
　 ⅛　t.　salt
3　large eggs
4　T.　sugar
oil

❶ Sift flour twice.
❷ Bring ① to a boil; slowly add it to the flour and mix until smooth. Add eggs one at a time; beat lightly into a smooth heavy batter.
❸ Heat the pan then add the oil; heat the oil to medium hot. Squeeze one portion of the batter into a ball (¹⁄₁₆); scoop out the ball with a greased spoon (Fig. 1) then put it into the oil (Fig. 2). Scoop out the other 15 balls in the same manner. Deep-fry over medium heat until the balls have tripled in size; turn heat to high and cook until golden (Fig. 3). The total frying time should be about 7 minutes. Remove and drain; coat with sugar.
■ The puffs may be served with jam or jelly.

　 { 糖‥‥‥‥‥‥‥‥‥‥‥‥ ⅔杯
① { 猪油‥‥‥‥‥‥‥‥‥‥‥ 1大匙
　 { 雞蛋‥‥‥‥‥‥‥‥‥‥‥ 2個
② { 麵粉‥‥‥‥‥‥‥‥‥‥‥ 2杯
　 { 發粉‥‥‥‥‥‥‥‥‥‥‥ 1小匙
白芝麻‥‥‥‥‥‥‥‥‥‥‥ ½杯
「炸油」‥‥‥‥‥‥‥‥‥‥‥ 適量

❶將①料攪拌均匀，倒入篩過之②料略攪拌，輕揉成麵糰，分切成16塊（圖4），沾水揉成球形（圖5）再滾上芝麻（圖6），用手輕揉芝麻球使芝麻陷入麵糰，炸時才不會掉落。
❷「炸油」略燒熱，放入麵球，小火炸至裂開口即改大火炸呈金黄色撈出，待冷後香甜而酥。
■因炸後麵球裂開如同開口笑，表示吉祥，故常用來做年節的點心。

"Open Mouth Laugh" Makes 16

　 { ⅔　c.　sugar
① { 1　T　lard or shortening
　 { 2　large eggs
② { 2　c.　flour
　 { 1　t.　baking powder
　 ½　c.　sesame seeds
oil

❶ Mix ingredients of ① until thoroughly combined; sift ② and add to ①. Knead to a soft dough; flatten the dough slightly and cut it into 16 pieces (Fig. 4). Dip a piece of dough in water and roll it into a ball (Fig. 5). Roll the ball in the sesame seeds (Fig. 6). Be sure to press the seeds slightly into the balls so that the seeds won't fall off during frying. Make the other balls in the same manner.
❷ Heat the wok to medium hot then add oil; deep-fry the balls over low heat until they expand and open. Turn the heat to high and deep-fry the balls until golden brown; remove, drain and let cool. Serve.
■ The balls open like a smiling face. This dish is usually served at festive occasions.

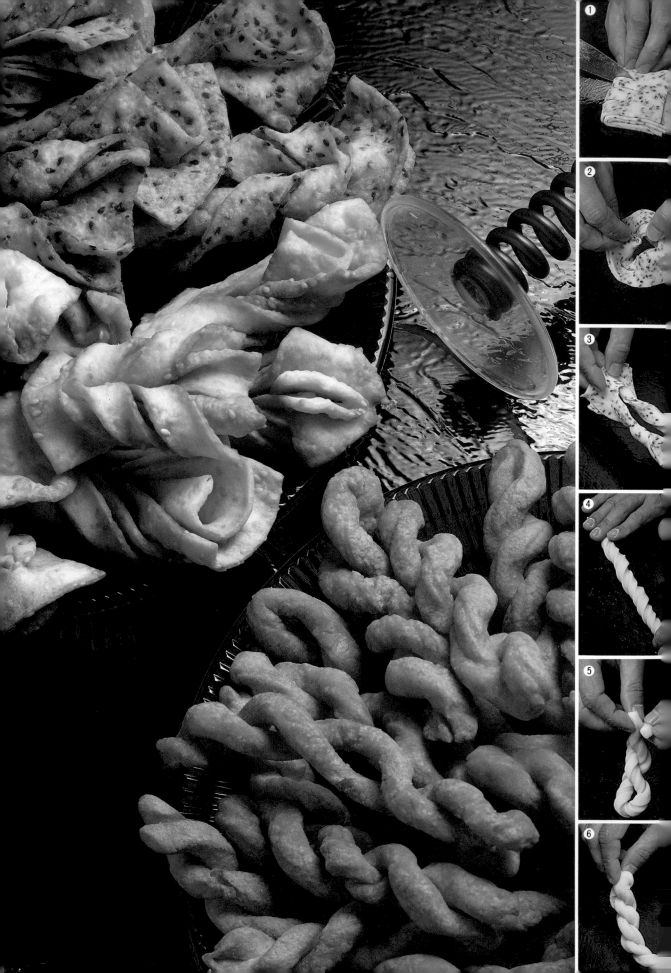

①
- 細砂糖‥‥‥‥‥‥‥½杯
- 黑或白芝麻‥‥‥‥‥¼杯
- 豆腐（壓碎）‥‥‥‥½杯
  （或奶水⅓杯加發粉1小匙）
- 雞蛋‥‥‥‥‥‥‥‥1個
- 塩‥‥‥‥‥‥‥‥‥⅛小匙

麵粉‥‥‥‥‥‥‥‥‥‥2杯
「炸油」‥‥‥‥‥‥‥‥適量

❶將①料拌至糖溶化後，隨加入篩過的麵粉，揉成十分光滑的麵糰，如太硬或太軟時，酌量加入水或麵粉揉成軟硬適中之麵糰，擱置半小時（俗稱醒麵）。

❷將麵糰趕成大薄片（越薄炸出的巧菓越脆）再切成長9公分，寬4公分之長方形，對折，中間切三條刀痕（圖1），每片由一端穿過中間切口拉直（圖2.3.）。

❸「炸油」燒熱，放入巧菓用中火炸3分鐘至金黃色撈出待冷香脆可口。（分數次炸）

■將巧菓裝入罐內蓋緊，可保存數星期。

Chiao Gwo　　Makes 30 strips

①
- ½ c. sugar
- ¼ c. sesame seeds
- ½ c. bean curd (or ⅓ c. evoporated milk and 1 t. baking powder)
- 1 large egg
- ⅛ t. salt
- 2 c. sifted flour
- oil

❶ In a bowl, mix ① thoroughly until sugar is dissolved. Gently add sifted flour, mix, and knead it into a soft dough. If the dough is too dry, add water; if too moist, add flour. Knead until the dough is smooth and velvety; let it stand for 30 minutes.

❷ Roll the dough into a thin sheet. The thinner it is, the crispier it will fry. Cut the sheet into rectangular shapes, 3½"x1½". Place 2 rectangular pieces of dough on top of each other. At the short end, fold the rectangles in half then cut 3 equally spaced slits (Fig. 1). Unfold the strips. Take the short end of the strip and pass it through the middle slit (Fig. 2) and pull it to the full length (Fig. 3). Make the remaining strips in the same manner.

❸ Heat the oil; deep-fry the strips, "Ch'iao Gwo", over low heat for 3 minutes or until they are golden brown; remove and let cool. Serve.

Ch'iao Gwo will keep fresh for several weeks if they are stored in an air-tight glass container.

①
- 蛋‥‥‥‥‥‥‥‥‥‥2個
- 糖‥‥‥‥‥‥‥‥‥‥½杯
- 塩‥‥‥‥‥‥‥‥‥‥¼小匙
- 小蘇打或發粉‥‥‥‥1小匙

麵粉‥‥‥‥‥‥‥‥‥‥2杯
「炸油」‥‥‥‥‥‥‥‥適量

❶將①料拌至糖溶化後，隨加入篩過的麵粉，揉成十分光滑的麵糰，如太硬或太軟時，酌量加入水或麵粉揉成軟硬適中之麵糰，擱置半小時（俗稱醒麵）。

❷將麵糰趕成長方形狀（24公分×15公分×0.5公分），並分切成24條。

❸取一條麵條左手拉住一端，用右手輕壓另一端向前搓滾（圖4），將麵條提起兩端捏合（圖5），再扭成麻花狀（圖6）。

❹「炸油」燒熱，放入麻花用中火炸4分鐘至金黃色撈出待冷香脆可口。

■將麻花裝入罐內蓋緊，可保存數星期。

Crispy Twists　　Makes 24

①
- 2 large eggs
- 2 c. flour
- ½ c. powdered sugar
- ¼ t. salt
- 1 t. baking soda or baking powder
- 2 c. sifted flour
- oil

❶ In a bowl, mix ① thoroughly until sugar is dissolved; add flour, knead it into a soft dough. If the dough is too dry, add water; if too moist, add flour. Knead the dough until it is smooth; let it sit for 30 minutes.

❷ Roll the dough into a thin sheet (10"x3"x⅕"); cut the sheet into 24 pieces.

❸ Use one hand to take a piece of dough and lightly stretch the strip while the other hand holds the opposite end firmly pressed on the table. Twist the strip to form a spiral (Fig. 4). Bring both ends of the twisted strips together (Fig. 5) and twist them (Fig. 6) so that the ends connect. Make the other twists in the same manner.

❹ Heat the wok then add oil. Deep-fry the twists over medium heat for 4 minutes or until they are golden brown. Remove, drain and cool. Serve.

■ Crispy twists will keep fresh for several weeks if they are stored in an air-tight glass container.

鹹碗粿　　　　8個

① { 在萊米粉（粘米粉）‥1½杯
　　水‥‥‥‥‥‥‥‥3杯
　　塩‥‥‥‥‥‥‥‥½小匙

② { 炸紅葱頭‥‥‥‥‥2大匙
　　胡椒‥‥‥‥‥‥½小匙
　　塩‥‥‥‥‥‥‥¼小匙

蘿蔔乾（切碎）‥‥‥‥‥‥1兩
絞肉‥‥‥‥‥‥‥‥‥‥2兩
小碗‥‥‥‥‥‥‥‥‥‥8個

❶ 將①料拌成米漿，用小火煮，煮時需不停的攪拌約3分鐘（圖1），煮成濃稠狀（圖2）。

❷ 油2大匙燒熱，將絞肉和蘿蔔乾放入炒香，拌入②料炒勻備用。

❸ 將米漿分盛在小碗內，盛八分滿，將炒香蘿蔔乾等撒在上面（圖3），以大火蒸30分鐘至熟即可。食時加些醬油、辣椒醬、香菜等。

甜碗粿　　　　8個

① { 在萊米粉（粘米粉）‥‥‥‥‥‥1½杯
　　細砂糖‥‥‥‥‥‥‥‥‥‥‥⅔杯
　　水‥‥‥‥‥‥‥‥‥‥‥‥‥3杯

小碗‥‥‥‥‥‥‥‥‥‥‥‥‥8個

❶ 同上做法❶。

❷ 將米漿分盛在小碗內，盛八分滿，以大火蒸30分鐘至熟即可。

Salty Steamed Rice Pudding
Serves 8

① { 1½ c. rice flour
　　3 c. water
　　½ t. salt
　　¼ c. dried turnip
　　⅛ lb. ground meat, beef or pork

② { 2 T. shallots
　　½ t. black pepper
　　¼ t. salt
8 small bowls

❶ Mix ① until very smooth; cook ① over low heat (Fig. 1) while stirring continuously for about 3 minutes or until it is thick (Fig. 2). Set rice batter aside.

❷ Heat the wok then add 2 T. oil. Stir-fry ground meat and turnip until they become fragrant. Add ② and stir well.

❸ Portion rice batter into 8 small bowls; spoon the turnip mixture on top of the rice batter (Fig. 3). Place the bowls in a steamer and steam over high heat for 30 minutes. Remove and serve with soy sauce, hot bean paste and coriander.

Sweet Steamed Rice Pudding
Serves 8

① { 1½ c. rice flour
　　⅔ c. granulated sugar
　　3 c. water
8 small bowls

❶ Same as step ❶ of "Salty Steamed Rice Pudding".

❷ Portion rice batter into 8 small bowls. Place in a steamer and steam over high heat for 30 minutes; remove and serve.

發糕　　　　8個

① { 在萊米粉（粘米粉）‥‥‥‥3杯
　　糖（紅、白糖均可）‥‥‥1杯
　　水‥‥‥‥‥‥‥‥‥‥1½杯

② { 麵粉‥‥‥‥‥‥‥‥‥‥¾杯
　　發粉‥‥‥‥‥‥‥‥‥1大匙

小碗‥‥‥‥‥‥‥‥‥‥8個

❶ 將①料內的水、糖先溶化（圖4）。倒入在萊米粉內（圖5）攪勻，隨加入過篩的②料（圖6）一起攪拌均勻，分盛在小碗內，盛八分滿，待蒸。

❷ 水燒開，將小碗排在蒸盤內，大火蒸30分鐘至熟，待冷即可取出。食時，可切片煎來吃或蒸熱吃。

■ 做發糕時也可加入各種果汁粉做成各種不同味道及顏色的發糕。

■ 發糕蒸熟時會脹發裂開口，暗示新的一年將發大財，此為年節的點心，取其吉祥的象徵。

> 如無在萊米粉，可取相同份量的在萊米加水泡六小時後，用菓汁機打碎成米漿再使用。

Steamed Rice Cupcakes
Serves 8

① { 3 c. rice flour
　　1 c. sugar (brown or white)
　　1½ c. water

② { ¾ c. flour
　　1 T. baking powder
　　8 small bowls

❶ Dissolve 1 cup sugar in 1½ cups water in a mixing bowl (Fig. 4). Add the water to rice flour and mix well (Fig. 5); add sifted ingredients in ② (Fig. 6) and stir until thoroughly mixed. Portion the batter into the small bowls.

❷ Place the bowls in a steamer and steam over boiling water for about 30 minutes. Allow the cakes to cool then remove them from steamer. Slice the cakes and fry or steam them when ready to serve.

■ Fruit flavor gelatin may be added for color and taste.

■ These cakes are usually served at New Year for festive occasion.

> If rice flour is unavailable, soak 3 cups long-grained rice in water for 6 hours then blend it in a blender until very fine.

蘿蔔糕 1份

① { 在萊米粉（粘米粉）…………4杯
　　水………………………………3杯 }
② { 白蘿蔔絲……………………2斤
　　水………………………………1杯 }
③ { 塩……………………………1½小匙
　　胡椒…………………………1小匙 }
蒸盤（27公分×30公分×6公分）‥1個
玻璃紙（36公分×39公分）………1張

❶將①料攪勻成米漿。蒸盤內舖上玻璃紙備用。

❷②料置鍋內，蓋鍋，用小火煮20分鐘至蘿蔔絲呈透明且爛（圖1），即把③料和米漿倒入（圖2）繼續以小火煮至半熟，煮時翻拌以免燒焦（圖3）。倒入蒸盤內並抹平，以大火蒸40分鐘，插入筷子試試，見不粘筷時即成。

臘味蘿蔔糕

蘿蔔糕內多加入臘味即成「臘味蘿蔔糕」。

臘味做法：蝦米1兩、紅葱頭3大匙，香腸與臘肉各3兩切丁，一同炒香，與米漿等一齊倒入蘿蔔絲內混合，其他做法與「蘿蔔糕」同。

Steamed Turnip Cake

① { 4 c. rice flour }
　　3 c. water } mix
② { 2⅔ lbs. pared, shredded turnip
　　1 c. water }
③ { 1½ t. salt
　　1 t. black pepper }
baking pan (10⅝"x12"x2⅜")
1 sheet plastic wrap (14"x15")

❶ Mix ① together well to prepare the batter. Line the baking pan with plastic wrap.

❷ Put ② in a pan; cover and cook 20 minutes over low heat until soft (Fig. 1). Add ③ and rice flour mixture (Fig. 2).Cook for 5 minutes and stir continuously so that mixture does not stick to the pan or burn (Fig. 3). Pour into the steamer. Smooth the top and steam for 40 minutes. Test for doneness with a toothpick. Let cool and slice.

Spicy Steamed Turnip Cake

Use ingredients ①, ②, ③, pan and plastic wrap of Steamed Turnip Cake.
Stir-fry 1 oz. chopped dried shrimp, 3 T. fried shallots, and ¼ lb. each of Chinese sausage and Chinese bacon; add this mixture and flour batter to the turnip; mix well. Continue to follow steps ❶ and ❷ of steamed Turnip Cake.
Sliced turnip cake may be fried.

倫教糕 1份

① { 在萊米粉（粘米粉）…………3杯
　糖……………………………1½杯
　水………………………………3杯 }
② { 酵母粉…………………………½大匙
　温水……………………………2大匙 }
蒸盤（27公分×30公分×6公分）‥1個
玻璃紙（36公分×39公分）………1張

❶①料內加入在萊米粉，拌勻成「米漿」。②料攪拌後擱置10分鐘。蒸盤內舖玻璃紙備用。

❷米漿用小火煮成濃稠狀，煮時需不停攪拌以免結硬塊或燒焦，然後用篩子過濾（圖4）。待冷後加入酵母水拌勻（圖5），置6～8小時至表面起很多氣泡（圖6）即倒入蒸盤內，用大火蒸25分鐘至熟，待冷切塊食用。倫教糕因發酵過，所以有特別的酵母香味及自然酸味，非常爽口而不膩。

如無在萊米粉，可取相同份量的在萊米加水泡六小時後，用菓汁機打碎成米漿再使用。

Steamed Rice Cake

① { 3 c. rice flour
　1½ c. sugar
　3 c. water }
② { ½ t. yeast
　2 T. warm water }
baking pan (10⅝"x12"x2⅜")
1 sheet plastic wrap (14"x15")

❶ Add ① to rice flour; mix well to prepare the batter. Mix ② and let stand for 10 minutes. Line the baking pan with the sheet of plastic wrap.

❷ Cook the batter over low heat until it has thickened. Stir continuously during cooking so that the batter does not stick to the pan or burn. Pour the batter through a sieve into a bowl (Fig. 4). Add ② to the batter and mix well (Fig. 5); let stand for 6 to 8 hours or until the bubbles form (Fig. 6). Pour the batter into the baking pan; steam over high heat for 25 minutes or until cooked. Allow to cool before cutting; serve.

If rice flour is unavailable, soak 3 cups long-grained rice in water for 6 hours then blend it in a blender until very fine.

① 在莱米粉(粘米粉)⋯⋯⋯3杯
　澄麵或太白粉⋯⋯⋯⋯⋯¾杯
　水⋯⋯⋯⋯⋯⋯⋯⋯⋯6杯
蒸盤(21公分×33公分)⋯⋯⋯1個
油⋯⋯⋯⋯⋯⋯⋯⋯⋯⋯2大匙

❶①料拌匀成「米漿」。
❷燒滾半大鍋水,將蒸盤抹油放在沸水上,倒入米漿¾杯
　(圖1)隨即輕晃盤子(圖2)使米漿厚薄均匀,蓋鍋,
　大火蒸5分鐘見表面凝固微起泡即熟,取出待涼即為
　「河粉」(圖3)。
■如無在莱米粉,可取相同份量的在莱米加水泡六小時
　後,用菓汁機打碎成米漿再加澄麵拌匀使用。
■做好的河粉可做三絲腸粉捲,或切絲做河粉湯、炒河
　粉等。

Rice Sheet ("Sha Her Fen")
Makes 10

① 3　c.　rice flour*
　¾　c.　cornstarch
　6　c.　water
　baking pan (8"x13")
　2　T.　oil

❶ Mix ① well to prepare the batter.
❷ Boil water in a half filled steamer. Grease the baking
pan with oil then place it in the steamer. Pour the ¾
cup of batter into the pan (Fig. 1). Shake the pan
slightly to distribute the batter evenly (Fig. 2). Cover
and steam over high heat for 5 minutes or until the top
of the batter become slightly firm and begins to
bubble; remove. Repeat steaming process for the
remaining rice sheets. Allow to cool; remove and
serve.
◂ If rice flour is unavailable, soak 3 cups long-grained
rice in water for 6 hours then blend it in a blender until
it is very fine.
◂ Rice sheet may be used for "Three-shred Rice Rolls" or
may be shredded to stir-fry or to make soup.

沙河粉⋯⋯⋯⋯⋯⋯⋯⋯6張
肉絲(牛、豬或雞)⋯⋯⋯⋯6兩
① 太白粉⋯⋯⋯⋯⋯⋯½大匙
　醬油、料酒⋯⋯⋯各1大匙
香菇絲⋯⋯⋯⋯⋯⋯⋯⋯¼杯
榨菜絲⋯⋯⋯⋯⋯⋯⋯⋯1杯
② 糖⋯⋯⋯⋯⋯⋯⋯⋯1小匙
　胡椒⋯⋯⋯⋯⋯⋯⋯¼小匙

❶肉絲加①料拌匀略醃。油3大匙燒熱,將肉絲炒熟,
　入香菇略炒,再加榨菜及②料一同炒拌1分鐘即為「
　餡」。
❷每張沙河粉放兩堆餡,捲成兩個三絲腸粉(圖4.5.6.)
　共可做12捲。放在蒸盤內蒸2分鐘,趁熱依喜好酌加
　醬油、辣椒醬、香菜等食之。
■榨菜很鹹需先泡水10分鐘後擠乾水份再用。
　餡可隨個人嗜好改用其他材料,如蝦、筍、韮黃等。

Three-shred Rice Rolls
Makes 12

　6　rice sheets ("sha her fen")
　½　lb. shredded meat (beef, pork, or chicken)
① ½　T.　cornstarch
　1　T.　each: soy sauce, cooking wine
　¼　c.　pre-softened, shredded Chinese black
　　　mushrooms
　1　c.　shredded Szechuan pickled mustard greens
② 1　t.　sugar
　¼　t.　pepper
　oil

❶ Mix the meat and ① thoroughly, marinate for 5
minutes. Heat the wok then add 3 T. oil; stir-fry the
meat until cooked. Add the mushrooms; stir lightly.
Add Szechuan pickled mustard greens and ②; stir for
1 minute. This is the filling. Divide the filling into 12
equal portions.
❷ Two rice rolls are made from each rice sheet. Spoon
one portion along the short end of the rice sheet and
one portion just above the half of the rice sheet. Roll
up the lower end to a baton-like shape (Figs. 4, 5).
Cut the rice sheet (Fig. 6) and form the next roll. Make
the remaining rolls in the same manner. Place the rolls
in a steamer and steam for 2 minutes. Serve hot with
soy sauce, hot bean paste or coriander.
■ Szechuan pickled mustard greens should be soaked
in water for ten minutes. Squeeze out the water before
using. Shrimp, bamboo shoots, yellow Chinese chives
may be used as filling.

糯米粉‥‥‥‥‥‥‥‥‥‥6杯

①{
糖‥‥‥‥‥‥‥‥‥‥‥1杯
溫水‥‥‥‥‥‥‥‥‥‥2杯
食用紅粉（水）‥‥‥‥⅛小匙
}

紅豆沙或綠豆沙餡‥‥‥（1斤）2杯

龜形粿模‥‥‥‥‥‥‥‥1個

蔬菜或植物葉子‥‥‥‥‥10個

❶餡：豆沙分成10等份。

❷皮：將①料拌勻，俟糖溶化後拌入糯米粉揉合成軟硬適度的粿糰，並分成10等份。

❸每一份粿糰揉成極光滑，並捏成凹圓狀，中間放入豆沙餡包成圓球狀。

❹龜模刷上一層油，把做好的粿球放入（圖1），在模型內壓平（圖2），打開模把印好的紅龜倒在葉上（圖3）將葉子略修剪。

❺水燒開，將紅龜置蒸盤上大火蒸10分鐘至熟透取出，抹上少許油以免表面乾硬，冷吃熱食均宜。

■做好龜粿放入冰箱可保存一星期，但冰過的龜粿變硬食時需蒸熱或煎熱。

■「龜」本象徵長壽，故一般都喜以大紅色的紅龜粿來慶賀大壽。

■紅豆沙做法參照第13頁。

Turtle-shaped Glutinous Rice Cakes

Makes 10

```
6   c. glutinous flour
  { 1   c. suggar
① { 2   c. warm water
  { ⅛   t.  red food coloring
  2   c. red bean paste*
  1   turtle shape mold
  10  lemon or similar leaves
```

❶ Filling: Divide red bean paste into 10 portions.

❷ Skin: In a bowl, mix ① until sugar is dissolved; add glutinous flour and mix to form dough. Divide the dough into 10 portions. Knead each portion until smooth then press them to form concave round shapes.

❸ Place 1 portion of filling in the center of the dough and gather the edges of the dough to enclose the filling. Pinch to seal and roll into a ball.

❹ Grease the mold with oil. Place a dough ball on the mold (Fig. 1); press it into the mold to flatten it (Fig. 2). Open the mold and let the molded dough fall on a leaf (Fig. 3). Trim the leaf. Follow steps ❸ and ❹ for the remaining dough.

❺ Steam the cakes over boiling water for 10 minutes or until they are cooked. Remove. Lightly oil the top of the cakes to prevent them from becoming hard and dry. These cakes may be served either hot or cold. The cakes may be stored in a refrigerator and will keep for 1 week. Refrigerated cakes should be fried or steamed before serving.

■ The turtle represents long life, so these cakes are usually served at a birthday party or other special occasions.

■ See p. 13 for directions to prepare red bean paste.

餡：蘿蔔絲‥‥‥‥‥‥‥1斤

鹽‥‥‥‥‥‥‥‥‥‥‥2小匙

豬肉‥‥‥‥‥‥‥‥‥‥6兩

①{
蒜‥‥‥‥‥‥‥‥‥‥1大匙
蝦米‥‥‥‥‥‥‥‥‥4大匙
}

②{
醬油‥‥‥‥‥‥‥‥‥1大匙
胡椒‥‥‥‥‥‥‥‥‥⅛小匙
}

青菜葉或水菓葉‥‥‥‥‥16片

皮：

③{
糯米粉‥‥‥‥‥‥2½杯
在萊米粉‥‥‥‥‥‥1杯
}

④{
溫水‥‥‥‥‥‥‥1¼杯
豬油‥‥‥‥‥‥‥1大匙
}

❶餡：蘿蔔絲加鹽2小匙醃15分鐘後擠乾水份。豬肉切絲備用。油4大匙燒熱，將①料炒香，隨入肉絲爆香即可放入蘿蔔絲及②料炒勻盛起，待冷分成16份。

❷皮：③料篩過後，加入④料揉成光滑且軟硬適度之糯米糰（米糰太硬或太軟時可酌量加水或糯米粉）。分切16小塊。

❸每小塊糯米糰按扁成圓薄片，若黏手可塗些油，將餡置中央包好放在青菜葉上（圖4. 5. 6.）。將菜包粿置蒸盤上，大火蒸15分鐘至熟，即可趁熱食之。

■除蘿蔔絲外也可用高麗菜來做。

Steamed Vegetable Dumplings

Makes 16

```
Filling:
   1⅓ lbs. pared, shredded turnips
   2   t.  salt
   ½   lb. shredded pork
① { 1   T.  sliced garlic
  { 4   T.  dried shrimp
② { 1   T.  soy sauce
  { ⅓   t.  pepper
   16  lemon, cabbage or similar leaves
Skin:
③ { 2½  c. glutinous rice flour
  { 1   c. rice flour
④ { 1¼  c. warm water
  { 1   T. lard
```

❶ Filling: Mix the turnips with 2 t. salt and let it sit for 15 minutes; squeeze out the excess water. Heat the wok then add 4T. oil. Stir-fry ① until fragrant. Add the pork then the turnip and ②, stir-fry to mix together. Remove and allow to cool. Divide into 16 portions.

❷ Skin: Sift ingredients of ③ together. Add the water of ④ and mix well; add lard of ④ and mix well. Knead to a smooth dough and cut into 16 pieces.

❸ Flatten a piece of dough into circles (if sticky, add a little oil). Place some filling in the center of the dough (Fig. 4) and fold it in half. Pinch the edges to seal (Fig. 5). Make the other dumplings in the same manner. Place each finished dumpling on a leaf (Fig. 6) and place in steamer. Steam for 15 minutes over high heat; serve.

■ Cabbage may be substituted for turnip.

紅豆年糕

小紅豆……………………………6兩
糖………………………………½杯
糯米粉……………………………6杯
① { 糖（紅糖、白糖均可）………2杯
　　熱水……………………………2½杯
蒸盤（27公分×30公分×6公分）‥1個
玻璃紙（36公分×39公分）…………1張

❶ **煮紅豆**：小紅豆洗淨，加水5杯浸泡6小時以上，用
大火煮開後，改小火，蓋鍋續煮至豆軟，但不裂開，
見水快乾時（圖1）（如水份仍多可改大火燒乾）再加糖
½杯（圖2）煮至糖溶化即可，為保持紅豆顆粒完整，
攪拌時不要用力（圖3）。

❷ ①料攪勻至糖溶化，待涼，倒入糯米粉拌合至全部均
勻，再拌入煮好的紅豆備用。

❸ 蒸盤內舖上玻璃紙，倒入拌勻糯米漿，水開蒸2小時
插入筷子試試，不粘筷時即可。
拌好的生紅豆米漿，也可直接放入油煎，小火兩面煎
黃約需3分鐘。

Red Bean New Year's Cake

½ lb. small red beans
½ c. sugar
6 c. glutinous rice flour
① { 2 c. sugar
　　2½ c. hot water
baking pan, 10⅝"x12"x2⅜"
1 sheet plastic wrap, 14"x15"

Rinse the beans then soak them in 5 cups water for at
least 6 hours. Cook the beans in water over high heat;
bring to a boil. Turn the heat to low; cover and cook
until the water has almost evaporated and the beans
are soft but not open (Fig. 1). If there is still a lot of
water remaining, turn the heat to high to evaporate
the water. Add ½ cup sugar (Fig. 2) and stir gently until
the sugar is dissolved. Stir lightly so that the beans do
not break apart (Fig. 3).

Stir ① until the sugar is dissolved; let cool. Add
glutinous rice flour to ① and mix thoroughly; add the
beans. This makes rice paste.

Line the baking pan with the sheet of plastic wrap.
Put the rice paste mixture into the pan; steam over
boiling water for 2 hours. Test for doneness with a
toothpick. OR Divide the rice paste into several
portions then fry it, one portion at a time, over low heat
for 3 minutes or until both sides are golden brown.

甜年糕

做法與材料均參照「紅豆年糕」，只是不加紅豆。

■ 剛蒸好的年糕很軟可馬上吃，或待一、二天後略
硬時切片煎或沾蛋糊炸來吃，亦可夾上酸菜、香
菜、花生粉等（圖4.5.6.）。年糕擱置時間愈久愈
硬，但加熱後即軟，放冰箱內可保存數星期不壞。

■ 年糕按地域的不同有各種不同的風味，通常都是
在過年前做好，在年節時慢慢享用，過去都是用
糯米泡水後再用石磨磨成米漿來做，尤其大家庭
每次製做份量多非常費時費事，現在市面上有磨
好的糯米粉出售，只要照份量拌好，放入電鍋內
蒸熟，非常簡單，隨時都可做。

Sweet New Year's Cake

Ingredients and procedures are the same as "Red Bean
New Year's Cake", except red beans are not used.

■ The cake can be served immediately after steaming
while it is soft. If the cake becomes hard one or two
days after steaming, it may be either sliced and fried,
or sliced, dipped in egg-flour paste, and deep-
fried. This cake may also be sliced sandwich style
(Fig. 4) and served with pickled mustard cabbage
(Fig. 5), coriander, or peanut butter powder (Fig. 6).
This cake may be stored in a refrigerator for several
weeks. The longer the cake is kept, the harder it will
become; however, heating will make it soft.

■ This cake has different flavors in different regions. It is
usually prepared before new year and served during
new year.

芝麻湯圓‥‥‥‥‥‥‥‥12粒	①	糖‥‥‥‥‥‥‥‥‥‥‥‥¹⁄₂杯
（參照「芝麻湯圓」做法）		酒釀‥‥‥‥‥‥‥‥‥‥3大匙
水‥‥‥‥‥‥‥‥‥‥‥‥5杯		橘子或水蜜桃（罐裝）‥‥‥1杯
		雞蛋（打散）‥‥‥‥‥‥‥2個

● 水5杯燒開後，放入湯圓煮熟，隨入①料，再燒開時倒入雞蛋並徐徐推動，使成蛋花，最後加入水菓罐即成。

芝麻湯圓　20粒

餡：黑芝麻‥‥‥‥‥‥‥1兩	皮	②	糯米粉‥‥‥‥‥‥1杯
①	板油（或猪油）‥2¹⁄₂大匙		温水‥‥‥‥‥‥³⁄₄杯
	細砂糖‥‥‥‥2¹⁄₂大匙		

● 餡：黑芝麻篩去砂塵，洗淨，小火炒乾後壓成粉末，加①料一同攪勻成餡，入冰箱冰約20分鐘，取出分成20份，並搓圓（圖1）。

② 皮：將②料揉合並揣勻成糯米糰，分切爲20份。

③ 每份糯米糰包上餡，做成湯圓（圖2.3.）。水5杯燒開下湯圓煮5分鐘，見湯圓浮出水面即可盛碗食用。

■ 餡除黑芝麻外亦可用花生、豆沙等來做。

Sweet Rice Balls with Fermented Rice Wine

12 sweet rice balls (See "Sweet sesame Rice Ball Soup" for directions)
5 c. water
{ ¹⁄₂ c. sugar
{ 3 T. fermented rice wine (酒釀)
1 c. canned oranges or peaches
2 beaten eggs

Bring 5 c. water to a boil; add the rice balls and cook them. Add ① and bring to a boil; add the eggs and stir lightly. Add the canned oranges and serve.

Sweet Sesame Rice Ball Soup
Makes 20

Filling:
{ 1¹⁄₂ oz. black sesame seeds*
{ 2¹⁄₂ T. pork fat
{ 2¹⁄₂ T. confectioners sugar
Skin:
{ 1 c. glutinous rice powder
{ ³⁄₄ c. warm water

Filling: Rinse the sesame seeds; put the seeds in a greaseless pan and roast them over low heat until they are fragrant (about 30 seconds). Remove and grind the roasted seeds into a fine powder. Mix black sesame seed powder with ① until smooth. Refrigerate until solid, about 20 minutes; Remove and cut into 20 pieces. Roll each piece into a ball (Fig. 1).
Skin: Mix ingredients of ② into a smooth dough; roll the dough into a long roll and cut into 20 pieces. Roll each piece of dough into a ball; use the palm of the hand to flatten each piece of dough into a concave dough circle (Fig. 2). Place 1 portion filling in the center of dough circle (Fig. 3). Gather the edges around filling and pinch to seal. Roll the filled dough into a ball. Make the other rice balls in the same manner. Bring 5 cups water to a boil; add the balls and cook them over medium heat for 5 minutes or until they rise to the surface; pour the soup and balls into serving bowl and serve.
Peanuts or red bean paste may be substituted for the sesame seeds. See p. 13 for direction to make red bean paste.

餡：絞肉‥‥‥‥‥‥‥‥4兩	葱段3公分‥‥‥‥‥‥‥6支
①	炸香紅葱頭‥‥‥1大匙	③	清水‥‥‥‥‥‥‥‥9杯
	太白粉‥‥‥‥‥1小匙		塩‥‥‥‥‥‥‥‥2小匙
	塩‥‥‥‥‥‥¹⁄₃小匙		麻油‥‥‥‥‥‥1小匙
	麻油‥‥‥‥‥¹⁄₂小匙		胡椒‥‥‥‥‥¹⁄₄小匙
	胡椒‥‥‥‥‥¹⁄₄小匙	唐好菜‥‥‥‥‥‥‥‥4兩
皮	②	糯米粉‥‥‥‥‥2杯	
		温水‥‥‥‥‥‥³⁄₄杯	

● 餡：將絞肉加①料拌勻成餡，分成20份。

● 皮：將②料揉合並揣勻成糯米糰，分成20份。

● 將每份糯米糰用手捏成圓薄片，包上1份餡並捏合（圖4.5.6.）。

　油4大匙燒熱，將葱段炒香，隨下③料燒開，放入鹹湯圓，待滾約5分鐘見湯圓浮出水面，加唐好菜熄火即可供食。

■ 湯內可依喜好加入蝦米、蒜苗等以增香味。

Salty Rice Ball Soup
Makes 20

Filling:
¹⁄₈ lb. chopped pork
{ 1 T. minced, sauteed shallots
{ 1 t. cornstarch
① { ¹⁄₃ t. salt
{ ¹⁄₂ t. sesame oil
{ ¹⁄₄ t. pepper
Skin:
② { 2 c. glutinous rice powder
{ ³⁄₄ c. warm water
6 1-inch pieces of green onion
{ 9 c. water
③ { 2 t. salt
{ 1 t. sesame oil
{ ¹⁄₄ t. pepper
¹⁄₃ lb. "tang hau tsai" (or other green vegetable)

❶ Filling: Mix ① and chopped pork until ingredients are thoroughly combined; separate into 20 portions.
❷ Skin: Mix ingredients of ② and knead into a smooth rice dough; roll into a long roll and separate into 20 pieces.
❸ Shape each piece of dough into a circle (Fig. 4); place 1 portion filling in the center of the circle (Fig. 5). Gather the edges of the dough to enclose the filling. Pinch to seal (Fig. 6) or pinch edges then shape the filled dough into crescent shapes. Make the other rice balls in the same manner. Heat the pan then add 4 T. oil; stir-fry the onions until fragrant and add ③. Bring the liquid to a boil; add the rice balls and boil for 5 minutes over medium heat. When the rice balls rise to the surface, add green vegetable and turn off the heat; remove and serve.
■ Dried shrimp, fresh garlic, etc may be added to taste.

餡：紅豆沙……………… 1 ½杯
皮：糯米粉………………… 3杯
① { 糖………………………… ½杯
　　 水……………………… 1 杯
白芝麻…………………… 1 杯
「炸油」………………………適量

❶將豆沙分成20個餡。白芝麻洗淨晾乾備用。

❷皮：①料攪勻至糖完全溶化後再加入糯米粉，揉合成光滑且軟硬適度的麵糰（圖1），再揉成長條（圖2）分切成20小塊（圖3）。

❸每小塊糯米糰包入一份豆沙揉成圓球狀（圖4. 5. 6. ），沾水後再滾上芝麻，輕搓圓球使芝麻固定。

❹「炸油」略燒熱，放入糯米球，用中火炸呈金黃色且球脹大（5分鐘）即可撈出。

■紅豆沙做法參照第13頁。

Glutinous Rice Balls Makes 20

Filling:
1½ c. red bean paste*
Skin:
3 c. glutinous rice powder
① { ½ c. sugar
　　 1 c. water
1 c. white sesame seeds
oil

❶ Filling: Divide red bean paste into 20 portions.

❷ Skin: Mix ① until sugar is dissolved. Add glutinous rice flour to ① and knead into a smooth dough (Fig. 1). Roll the dough into a long roll (Fig. 2) and cut it into 20 pieces (Fig. 3).

❸ Flatten a piece of dough into a 2-inch concave dough (Fig. 4). Place a portion of filling in center (Fig. 5) and gather the edges of the dough to enclose the filling (Fig 6); pinch to seal. Roll the filled dough into a smooth ball; dip lightly in water, remove and coat with sesame seeds. Make the other balls in the same manner.

❹ Heat oil; deep-fry dough balls over medium heat for 5 minutes until expanded and golden. Remove, drain, and serve.

* See p. 13 for directions to prepare red bean paste.

餡：紅豆沙……………… 1 ½杯
皮：與「炸糯米球」同
沾料：椰蓉或花生粉………½杯

❶參照「糯米球」做法❶❷❸，包成圓球狀後，用大火蒸10分鐘至熟取出。

❷蒸好的熟糯米球沾水，用手搓至有黏性時沾裹沾料即成。

■紅豆沙做法參照第13頁。

Glutinous Rice Snowballs
Makes 20

Filling:
1½ c. red bean paste*
Skin: Same as for "Glutinous Rice Balls"
½ c. shredded coconut or peanut butter powder

❶ Follow steps ❶, ❷ and ❸ of "Glutinous Rice Balls" to "...roll the filled dough into a smooth ball...". Steam the dough balls over high heat for 10 minutes or until cooked; remove.

❷ Dip the steamed balls in water; remove. Roll the balls with the palm of the hand until sticky; coat the balls with coconut; serve.

* See p. 13 for directions to prepare red bean paste.

蓮藕⋯⋯⋯⋯⋯2斤左右	①	冰糖或砂糖⋯⋯⋯¾杯
糯米⋯⋯⋯⋯⋯1杯		煮藕汁⋯⋯⋯⋯⋯1杯
	②	太白粉⋯⋯⋯⋯1大匙
		水⋯⋯⋯⋯⋯2大匙

❶糯米洗淨，加水泡30分鐘後瀝乾水份，晾乾（或拭乾）
　水份後使用。

❷蓮藕刷洗乾淨，在每節蓮藕的一頭切下1吋長小塊，
　做為蓋子（圖1），用筷子通一通藕孔，將糯米填入孔
　內，邊填邊輕敲，將孔塞滿為止（圖2），再蓋上蓋子
　，用牙籤固定（圖3）。

❸做好的蓮藕加水（水需淹過蓮藕）用小火煮2小時半，
　取出，切0.5～1公分厚片，排入盤內。①料燒開後以
　②料勾芡淋在藕片上，趁熱食用。

■如一次吃不完，整條放在冰箱可保存幾天不壞，食時
　再切片，蒸熟淋上糖汁。

Sweet Lotus Root Filled with Glutinous Rice

2⅓ lbs. lotus roots
1 c. glutinous rice
① { ¾ c. rock sugar or brown sugar
　　1 c. retained lotus root liquid
② { 1 T. cornstarch
　　2 T. water } mix

❶ Rinse rice until water runs clear then soak it in water
for 30 minutes; drain.

❷ Wash and rinse lotus roots. Cut off a ½-inch section
from both ends of the roots (Fig. 1). Use a chopstick to
clean the holes of the root then fill the holes up with
rice (Fig. 2). Place the cut end piece on the rice filled
end to cover; secure in place with toothpicks (Fig. 3).

❸ Place the rice filled roots in a pan and add water to
cover the roots. Cook over low heat for 2½ hours;
remove the roots and retain the liquid. Slice the roots,
0.2-inch thick, and arrange them on a serving
plate. Bring ① to a boil; add mixture ② to thicken, stir
then pour it over the slices. Serve hot.

■ The rice-filled roots may be stored whole in the
refrigerator for at least 3 or 4 days. To serve, slice and
steam the roots. Bring ① to a boil; add ②, stir and pour
it over the slices.

餡：	里肌肉⋯⋯⋯⋯4兩		醬油⋯⋯⋯⋯½大匙
	蝦仁⋯⋯⋯⋯4兩		太白粉、麻油、糖⋯⋯⋯
①	太白粉⋯⋯⋯½大匙	②	各1小匙
	料酒⋯⋯⋯⋯1小匙		塩⋯⋯⋯⋯½小匙
	塩⋯⋯⋯⋯¼小匙		胡椒⋯⋯⋯⋯¼小匙
	香菇(切小丁)⋯⋯2朵		水⋯⋯⋯⋯½杯
	葱花⋯⋯⋯⋯1大匙	皮	糯米粉⋯⋯⋯3杯
			糖⋯⋯⋯⋯½杯
			水⋯⋯⋯⋯1杯
		「炸油」⋯⋯⋯⋯適量

❶餡：里肌肉、蝦仁切約1公分四方丁，加①料調勻，
　並炒熟。油4大匙燒熱，炒香葱花及香菇丁，隨加②
　料燒開，再放入炒熟的肉，蝦丁同炒勻成餡，待冷備
　用。

❷皮：參照第69頁「炸糯米球」做法❷。

❸每個糯米糰按扁成圓薄片（圖4），粘手時塗油，將餡
　置中央包好（圖5. 6.）。「炸油」燒熱，以中火炸，見鹹
　水餃浮出油面並呈金黃色脹大時（約需4分鐘）即可撈
　起。

Colden-fried Dumplings

Makes 20

Filling:
⅓ lb. pork loin
⅓ lb. raw, shelled shrimp
① { ½ T. cornstarch
　　1 t. cooking wine } mix
　　¼ t. salt
2 Chinese black mushrooms
1 T. chopped green onions
② { ½ T. soy sauce
　　1 t. each: cornstarch, sesame oil, sugar
　　½ t. salt
　　¼ c. pepper
　　½ c. water
oil

Skin:
③ { 3 c. glutinous rice flour
　　½ c. sugar
　　1 c. water

❶ Filling: Dice the pork and shrimp to ½-inch cubes;
mix with ①. Heat the pan then add 4 T. oil. Stir-fry the
pork and shrimp until the color changes; remove.
Reheat the pan and add 4 T. oil; stir-fry the green onions
and Chinese black mushrooms. Add ② and bring to
a boil; add the pork and shrimp and mix well.
Remove and allow to cool.

❷ Skin: Follow step ❷ of "Glutinous Rice Balls", p. 69.

❸ Flatten a piece of dough with the palm of the hand
(Fig. 4). Grease fingers lightly with a little oil if the
dough is sticky. Place one portion of the filling in the
center of the dough (Fig. 5); fold the dough in half and
pinch the edges to seal (Fig. 6). Make the other
dumplings in the same manner. Heat the oil for deep-
frying. Deep-fry ½ of the dumplings over medium heat
until they rise to the surface, are golden brown, and
have expanded about 4 times. Remove and
drain. Repeat step ❸ to make more dumplings; serve.

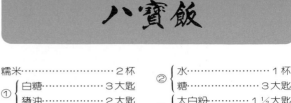

糯米‧‧‧‧‧‧‧‧‧‧‧‧‧‧‧‧‧‧‧‧‧‧‧‧‧‧‧‧3杯
① { 水‧‧‧‧‧‧‧‧‧‧‧‧‧‧‧‧‧‧‧‧‧‧‧‧1½杯
　　料酒‧‧‧‧‧‧‧‧‧‧‧‧‧‧‧‧‧‧‧‧4大匙
白糖或紅糖‧‧‧‧‧‧‧‧‧‧‧‧‧‧‧‧‧‧8兩
鋁盤（25公分×20公分×3公分）‧‧1個
玻璃紙（30公分×25公分）‧‧‧‧‧‧‧‧1張

❶糯米洗淨，加①料浸泡30分鐘，煮成糯米飯（參照「八
　寶飯」煮米法）。

❷煮熟糯米趁熱加糖拌勻（圖1）再用小火煮3分鐘至糖
　完全溶化且產生黏性時離火（圖2）。

❸鋁盤內先舖上玻璃紙，擦上少許油，倒入拌好的糯米
　飯，用飯勺或湯匙沾水壓平（圖3），待冷倒出切塊即
　可。

Glutinous Rice Cake

3 c. glutinous rice
1½ c. water
① { 4 T. cooking wine
⅔ lb. sugar
baking pan (10"x8"x1")
1 sheet plastic wrap (12"x10")

❶ Rinse the rice until the water runs clear then soak it in
① for 30 minutes; drain. Cook the rice (see "Eight-
treasure Rice Pudding" for direction to cook glutinous
rice)

❷ Add sugar to the cooked rice while it is hot; mix well
(Fig. 1). Cook the rice over low heat for 3 minutes or
until the sugar has dissolved (Fig. 2); remove from the
heat.

❸ Line the baking pan with a sheet of plastic wrap;
grease the sheet lightly with oil. Put the rice in the
pan. Dip a spatula or spoon in water to prevent the
rice from sticking to the spoon. Use the spoon to
smooth the surface of the rice (Fig. 3). Allow to cool
then cut it into pieces; serve.

糯米‧‧‧‧‧‧‧‧‧‧‧‧‧‧‧‧‧‧‧‧‧‧‧2杯　　　② { 水‧‧‧‧‧‧‧‧‧‧‧‧‧‧‧‧1杯
① { 白糖‧‧‧‧‧‧‧‧‧‧‧‧‧‧‧‧3大匙　　　　　糖‧‧‧‧‧‧‧‧‧‧‧‧‧‧3大匙
　　猪油‧‧‧‧‧‧‧‧‧‧‧‧‧‧‧‧2大匙　　　③ { 太白粉‧‧‧‧‧‧‧‧1½大匙
蜜餞（任選數種）‧‧‧‧‧‧‧1杯　　　　　　　水‧‧‧‧‧‧‧‧‧‧‧‧2小匙
豆沙‧‧‧‧‧‧‧‧‧‧‧‧‧‧‧‧‧‧‧‧‧‧3兩

❶糯米洗淨，煮成飯後，趁熱拌上①料。

❷備中碗1個，擦抹猪油1大匙後，把蜜餞排在碗底（
　圖4），先放一半拌好的糯米飯（圖5），中間略成凹狀，
　填入豆沙，再將另一半糯米飯舖蓋在豆沙上面並攤平
　，水開，大火蒸約1小時，取出後反扣圓盤內（圖6）。

❸②料燒開，以③料勾成糊狀，淋在八寶飯上即可。

糯米飯燒煮法：

2杯糯米洗淨，加1½杯水浸泡30分鐘後，用大火燒開
煮1分鐘，即改小火煮20分鐘，熄火，再燜10分鐘即可。
或用電鍋煮成糯米飯也可。

Eight-treasure Rice Pudding

2 c. glutinous rice
① { 3 T. sugar
2 T. lard or shortening
1 c. candied fruit of individual preference
¼ lb. red bean paste
② { 1 c. water
3 T. sugar
③ { 1½ T. cornstarch } mix
2 t. water

❶ Cook the rice as directed below; mix with ① while it
is still hot.

❷ Grease a heatproof bowl, 7"x3", with 1 T. lard or
shortening. Arrange the candied fruit in a circular
fashion as shown in (Fig. 4). Carefully place one half
of the rice on the fruit (Fig. 5). Pack the rice firmly so
that it lines the sides of the bowl. Leave an indentation
in the center of the rice; fill the middle with red bean
paste and add the rest of the rice to cover the bean
paste. Pack down the rice again. Use a spoon,
dipped in water, to make the surface smooth. Steam
the rice over high heat for 1 hour; remove. Place a
serving dish on the bowl and invert them to remove the
rice from the bowl (Fig. 6).

❸ Bring ② to a boil; add mixture ③ to thicken and
stir. Pour this syrup over the rice pudding and serve.

To cook glutinous rice:

Rinse 2 cups glutinous rice with water until the water
runs clear. Put 1½ cups of water in a pan; add the rice
and let it stand for about 30 minutes. Bring the water
to a boil over high heat; boil for 1 minute. Cover the
pan with a tight-fitting lid. Hereafter, do not uncover
rice until the cooking time has elapsed. Cook for 20
minutes over low heat; turn off the heat and let it stand
for 10 minutes. OR use a rice cooker to cook glutinous
rice:

肉　粽　10個

尖糯米	3杯		醬油	3大匙

尖糯米‧‧‧‧‧‧‧‧‧‧‧‧3杯
蝦米‧‧‧‧‧‧‧‧‧‧‧‧‧‧¼杯
① ┌ 醬油‧‧‧‧‧‧‧‧‧‧1½大匙
　├ 塩‧‧‧‧‧‧‧‧‧‧‧‧½小匙
　└ 胡椒‧‧‧‧‧‧‧‧‧‧¼小匙
腿肉‧‧‧‧‧‧‧‧‧‧‧‧‧½斤
香菇‧‧‧‧‧‧‧‧‧‧‧‧‧3朶
生鹹蛋黃‧‧‧‧‧‧‧‧‧5個

② ┌ 醬油‧‧‧‧‧‧‧‧‧‧3大匙
　├ 炸香紅葱頭片‧‧‧2大匙
　├ 料酒‧‧‧‧‧‧‧‧‧‧½大匙
　├ 糖‧‧‧‧‧‧‧‧‧‧‧‧1小匙
　└ 胡椒‧‧‧‧‧‧‧‧‧‧¼小匙
粽葉‧‧‧‧‧‧‧‧‧‧‧‧‧20張
粽繩‧‧‧‧‧‧‧‧‧‧‧‧‧10條

❶糯米洗淨，浸水約3小時後，瀝乾水份。粽葉、粽繩洗淨，在開水內煮約5分鐘，取出備用。

❷肉切爲20塊，香菇切10塊，加②料拌醃。鹹蛋也分切爲10塊，此即爲「餡」。

❸油4大匙燒熱，炒香蝦米，再下泡好的糯米及①料拌炒。

❹每二張粽葉折成三角形，包入糯米、肉、香菇、鹹蛋等料，再蓋上少許糯米，包成粽子，以粽繩繫好，放入鍋內（水需淹過粽子），水開，蓋鍋以小火續煮約1小時，至米完全熟透即可撈出。

■餡可依個人喜好改用其他各種材料。

Salty "Jungdz"　　Makes 10

3　c.　glutinous rice
¼　dried shrimp
① ┌ 1½　T.　soy sauce
　├ ½　t.　salt
　└ ¼　t.　pepper
⅔　lb.　pork flank or sliced bacon
3　Chinese black mushrooms
5　salty egg yolks
② ┌ 3　T.　soy sauce
　├ 2　T.　sliced, fried shallots
　├ ½　T.　cooking wine
　├ 1　t.　sugar
　└ ¼　t.　pepper

20　bamboo leaves
10　pieces of string

❶ Rinse the rice until the water runs clear then soak it in water for 3 hours; drain and divide it into 10 portions. Wash the bamboo leaves and strings then boil them for 5 minutes; remove and drain.

❷ Filling: Cut the pork and mushrooms into 20 pieces each; marinate them with ②. Cut each salty egg in half.

❸ Heat the pan then add 4 T. oil; stir-fry the dried shrimp until fragrant. Add the rice and ①; stir until mixed well.

❹ Lengthwise, overlap 2 leaves together then bend them to form a conical shape (To use as the wrapper), one end should be longer than the other. Put ½ portion of the rice and one piece each of the following in the conical — shaped leaves: pork black mushroom and salty egg. Cover ingredients with the other half of the rice. Wrap the leaves and tie them with a string. Follow the same step for the other "Jungdz". Place the finished "Jungdz" in a pot then add water to cover. Bring the water to a boil; turn the heat to low and cook the "jungdz" covered for 1 hour or until the rice is cooked; remove and serve.

■ The filling may be changed according to individual preference.

碱　粽　20個

① ┌ 圓糯米‧‧‧‧‧‧‧‧‧‧3杯
　└ 碱粉‧‧‧‧‧‧‧‧‧‧2½小匙
粽葉‧‧‧‧‧‧‧‧‧‧‧‧‧40張
粽繩‧‧‧‧‧‧‧‧‧‧‧‧‧20條

❶糯米洗淨，浸水約3小時，瀝乾水份，加碱粉拌勻。

❷每二張粽葉折成三角形，裝入3大匙的糯米，包時要注意留有空隙，不要裝滿，包成粽子，以粽繩繫緊。放入鍋內（水需淹過粽子），水開後改小火煮約2小時半，待冷即可沾糖、糖漿或蜂蜜食用。

■粽子包法：先將兩張粽葉對好（圖1），折成三角形（圖2），放入糯米（圖3），蓋好包成粽子狀（圖4），露出的葉子折好（圖5）以粽繩繫緊（圖6），用剪刀修去露出的粽葉梗。

Sweet "Jungdz"　　Makes 20

3　c.　glutinous rice
2½　t.　baking soda
40　bamboo leaves
20　pieces of string

❶ Filling: Rinse the rice until the water runs clear then soak it in water for 3 hours; drain. Mix the rice with baking soda.

❷ Lengthwise, overlap 2 leaves together and fold them into a conical shape (To use as the wrapper), one end should be longer than the other. Put 3 T. of the filling in the leaves. See below for directions to wrap the jungdz. Wrap the leaves loosely and tie them with string (filling will expand after cooking). Follow the same step for the other "jungdz". Place the "jungdz" in a pot then add water to cover. Bring the water to a boil; turn the heat to low and cook the "jungdz" for 2½ hours. Remove and allow to cool. Serve with sugar, syrup or honey.

■ Directions to wrap the "jungdz": Lengthwise, overlap 2 leaves together (Fig. 1) then bend them to form a conical shape (Fig. 2). Put the rice in the cone (Fig. 3). Fold the leaves over the rice and wrap the "jungdz" as shown (Figs. 4, 5). Tie the leaves with a string (Fig. 6). Cut off the ends of the leaves.

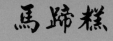

台式肉圓　　6個

肉絲·····½杯	②	地瓜粉或馬蹄粉·····2杯
筍絲·····1杯		太白粉·····½杯
香菇絲·····4大匙		水·····2杯
① 紅葱頭·····2大匙 糖、料酒·····各1大匙 醬油、麻油·····各1大匙 塩·····⅓小匙 五香粉·····¼小匙		「炸油」·····適量 沾料·····適量

❶油3大匙燒熱，先炒熟肉絲後，隨入筍、香菇絲及①料拌炒1分鐘成「餡」。

❷②料攪勻後用小火煮成半熟的濃稠狀（煮時需不停的攪動以免黏底或結硬塊）即成「粉漿」，注意不要煮太熟以免太硬。

❸飯碗內塗抹油，先舖3大匙粉漿於碗底，並用湯匙沾油抹成凹狀（圖1），中間放3大匙餡（圖2），最後再蓋上2大匙粉漿抹平（圖3），注意餡不要露出外面。

❹全部做好後移入蒸鍋內，大火蒸20分鐘至熟，待涼後取出肉丸直接淋上沾料食用。或將「炸油」燒熱，用小火泡炸後再淋沾料則味更香。

■沾料：可依個人喜好選用，甜麵醬、辣椒醬、辣糊醬蒜茸醬油、海鮮醬、香菜等。

Taiwanese-style Meat Pies

Makes 6

- ½ c. shredded meat, beef or pork
- 1 c. shredded bamboo shoots
- 4 T. shredded Chinese black mushrooms
- ① 2 T. shallots
  1 t. each: sugar, cooking wine
  1 T. each: soy sauce, sesame oil
  ⅓ t. salt
  ¼ t. five spices powder
- ② 2 c. sweet potato flour or water chestnut powder
  ½ c. cornstarch
  2 c. water
- oil
- dipping sauce*

❶ Filling: Heat a pan then add 3 T. oil; stir-fry the meat until it changes color. Add the bamboo shoots, black mushrooms and ①; stir-fry for 1 minute.

❷ Mix ② well then cook it over low heat until it thickens to become a thick batter; stir during cooking to prevent sticking. Do not overcook or the batter will be too hard.

❸ Grease a bowl with oil; spread 3 T. batter in the bottom of the bowl; grease a spoon with oil then use it to smooth the top of the batter and make a concave shape (Fig. 1). Place 3 T. filling in the center of the batter (Fig. 2) then cover the filling completely with 2 T. batter. Smooth the top of the batter (Fig. 3). Make the other pies in the same manner.

❹ Steam the finished meat pies over boiling water, over high heat, for 20 minutes or until they are cooked; allow to cool and remove. Serve with dipping sauce or deep-fry them over hot oil; use low heat. Serve with dipping sauce.

* Sweet bean paste, hot bean paste, soy sauce, hoisin sauce, etc. may be used as a dipping sauce.

馬蹄糕　　1份

①	馬蹄粉或地瓜粉·····2杯 水·····1½杯 奶水（濃縮）·····½杯
②	馬蹄（切絲）·····1杯 水·····2杯 糖·····1½杯
猪油·····2大匙	
蒸盤（27公分×30公分×6公分）·1個	
玻璃紙（36公分×39公分）·····1張	

❶蒸盤內舖上玻璃紙，並在玻璃紙上塗一層油備用。①料拌勻備用。②料燒開後徐徐倒入①料攪拌成濃稠狀，倒入蒸盤內，大火蒸30分鐘，待涼取出切片（圖1），鍋內放少許猪油將馬蹄糕以中火煎成金黃色（圖2.3.）趁熱食用。

■馬蹄即為荸薺。

Water Chestnuts Cake

- ① 2 c. water chestnut powder or sweet potato flour
  1½ c. water
  ½ c. evaporated milk
- ② 1 c. shredded water chestnuts
  2 c. water
  1½ c. sugar
- 2 T. lard or shortening
- baking pan (11"x12"x2")
- 1 sheet plastic wrap, 14"x15"

❶ Line a baking pan with plastic wrap; lightly grease the wrap with oil. In a bowl, mix ① well. Bring ② to a boil; pour ① slowly into ② and stir until thickened. Pour the mixture into the baking pan and steam it over high heat for 30 minutes; allow to cool. Remove the cake and slice it (Fig. 1). Fry the sliced cake in shortening, over medium heat, until the cake is slightly golden (Figs. 2,3). Remove and serve hot.

燒　餅　20個

麵粉‥‥‥‥‥‥‥‥6杯　　油酥‥‥‥‥‥‥‥‥¾杯

①{ 滾水‥‥‥‥‥‥1½杯　　塩‥‥‥‥‥‥‥‥½大匙
　 冷水‥‥‥‥‥‥½杯　　麵粉‥‥‥‥‥‥1大匙
　　　　　　　　　　　　白芝麻‥‥‥‥‥‥¼杯

❶把麵粉放在盆裏，將①料依次倒入，攪拌均勻，揉成光滑的麵糰。

❷將麵糰放在擦上油的案板上，用趕麵桿趕壓成45公分×45公分的四方麵片，然後把油酥均勻塗在麵片上，並撒上塩，再撒麵粉後，從麵片的一邊捲起，捲到盡頭成圓柱形，分切成20個小麵塊，將切口處兩端捏緊以免油酥流出。

❸把小麵塊橫放（兩端開口在左右）（圖1），從⅔處往前趕約10公分長（圖2），向前折二次翻面直放，從中間壓扁（圖3）向前折起，再從中間壓扁（圖4）又折起，在光滑面沾上白芝麻（圖5）輕壓緊，然後放直芝麻面朝下趕成15公分×8公分之長方形餅（圖6）。

❹將烤箱燒熱至350°F，燒餅芝麻面朝下，放入烤箱烤5分鐘後翻面再烤5分鐘呈金黃色即成。

■油酥做法：油1½杯燒熱，徐徐倒入3杯麵粉內（宜邊倒邊攪），用小火熬10分鐘，有香味呈淡咖啡色時離火（注意不可熬太焦，會有苦味），待冷即成油酥。

■做好的燒餅除單吃外，可夾油條、肉片或塗菓醬來吃。

Flaky Sesame Flat Breads ("Shau Bing")
Makes 20

6	c. flour	½	T. salt
1½	c. boiling water	1	T. flour
½	c. cold water	¼	c. white sesame seeds
¾	c. roux mixture *		

① (bracket covering first three ingredients)

❶ Place flour in a mixing bowl. Add the boiling water then the cold water of ① and mix well. Knead the mixture into a smooth, elastic dough.

❷ Lightly oil a surface to roll out the dough. Use a rolling pin to stretch the dough into a sheet, 1½ ft. square. Spread the surface of the square evenly with roux mixture and sprinkle with salt and flour. Roll up the square jelly-roll style; cut it into 20 pieces. Pinch the ends of each piece to keep the filling from spilling out.

❸ Place one piece of dough on the board, pinched edges on sides (Fig. 1). Place the rolling pin at the one-third mark of the dough; roll out the dough, away from you, to about 4-inches (Fig. 2). Fold the lower third up to the center and fold down the top third. Turn the folded dough vertically. Place the rolling pin at the vertical center and press the dough (Fig. 3); fold the dough in half again. Place the rolling pin at the vertical center of the dough and press it down again (Fig. 4); fold in half again. Dip the piece of dough, smooth side down, in sesame seeds (Fig. 5). Roll out the dough, sesame seeds side down, into a 6"x3" rectangular shape (Fig. 6). Follow the same step for the other pieces.

❹ Preheat oven to 350°F. Bake the breads on a cookie sheet, sesame seeds side down, for 5 minutes; turn the breads over and bake them for 5 minutes or until golden.

＊ To make roux mixture: Heat 1½ cups oil until very hot; slowly add 3 cups flour and stir to mix well. Cook the flour over low heat for 10 minutes until fragrant and lightly golden. Do not overcook the breads. Remove the breads and allow them to cool; serve.
Crispy Chinese Crullers, roast beef or jam may be placed in split Flaky Seasame Flat Breads and serve.

甜　豆　漿　6人份

黃豆‥‥‥‥‥‥‥‥‥‥‥‥半斤
糖‥‥‥‥‥‥‥‥‥‥‥‥‥2杯

❶黃豆洗淨用清水浸泡（需淹蓋黃豆面3倍以上，夏天約6～8小時，冬天約12～14小時)至黃豆膨脹2～2.5倍。

❷浸好之黃豆瀝乾水份，加7杯水分幾次放入果汁機內攪碎。

❸將打碎黃豆裝入清潔之白布袋內（紗布亦可），再加水8杯擠出汁除去豆渣，即爲「生豆漿」。

❹將生豆漿以中火燒滾後改小火繼續燒煮10分鐘（以去豆腥味）即成豆漿。加糖成甜豆漿。

Sweet Soybean Milk ("Do Jiang")
Serves 6

⅔　lb. soybeans
2　c. sugar

❶ Rinse soybeans until the water runs clear. Put the beans in a pot and add water. The water should be three times the amount of the soybeans. Soak the beans until they expand to 2 or 2½ times. In hot weather, soak the beans for 6 to 8 hours; in cold weather, soak the beans for 12 to 14 hours.

❷ Drain the beans and discard the soaking water; add 7 cups water. Blend the beans and water in several batches until the beans are finely blended.

❸ Place the beans and 8 cups water in a cheesecloth bag; squeeze out the liquid. Retain the liquid and discard the sediment left in the cheesecloth bag.

❹ Bring the retained soybean liquid to a boil over medium heat. Turn the heat to low and cook for 10 minutes to remove the strong taste from the beans. Add sugar to the soybean milk and serve.

油　條

高筋麵粉·················6杯
清水······················2杯

① {
碳酸銨············2小匙
（或發粉1大匙）
小蘇打············2小匙
明礬···········1½小匙
（如無可免用）
塩···········1½小匙
}

「炸油」···················適量

❶將①料放在盆內，加入清水略攪拌使完全溶解後，加入麵粉調勻，擱置15～20分鐘，將麵自四周圍拉起向中央揉和，使之滑潤，再擱置15～20分鐘，再拉一次如此三或四次，即已非常滑潤，把整塊麵糰翻面，再抹少許油以防皮乾，放置一小時後用塑膠布或玻璃紙包成長條，擱置約4小時即可使用。（若做大量時，可將麵糰分為1斤之麵塊，再一一包好）。

❷將麵糰打開放在案板上邊趕邊拉長（圖1），並趕成7公分寬，0.3公分厚之長條（圖2），再切成1公分寬之小條（圖3），每2小條疊起（圖4），用細棒順長條中央壓一下（圖5），用手指捏著兩端拉長（圖6），放在滾熱油鍋裏不停翻撥，待定型為止，炸至金黃色取出即成。

■炸好的油條通常是配豆漿當早點，也可夾入燒餅內食用。

Crispy Chinese Crullers ("You Tiau")

```
6   c.  (1⅓ lbs) high protein flour
2   c.  water
①  {
2   t.  ammonium bicarbonate or 1 T. baking powder
2   t.  baking soda
1½  t.  alum* (food grade)
1½  t.  salt
}
    oil
```

❶ Place ingredients of ① in a mixing bowl; add water and stir until the ingredients have dissolved. Add flour and mix well; let stand for 15-20 minutes. Use your hand to take some dough around edges and drop it into the center of the dough; let stand for 15-20 minutes. Continue to drop the dough in the center of the bowl 3 or 4 times until the dough is elastic and smooth. Turn the dough over and lightly coat the surface with oil so that the dough will stay moist. Let it stand for 1 hour. Remove the dough from the bowl and place it on a sheet of plastic wrap; wrap the dough and form it into a rectangular shape. Let it stand for 4 hours. If a large batch is made, cut the dough into several 1⅓ lbs. pieces then wrap each piece in a sheet of plastic wrap.

❷ Unwrap the dough. Use a rolling pin to roll the dough and stretch it into a long strip (Fig. 1). Roll the dough into a rectangular shape, 3" wide and ¹⁄₁₆" thick (Fig. 2). Crosswise cut the rectangular shaped dough into strips, ⅛" wide (Fig. 3). Put two strips on top of each other (Fig. 4); Use a thin rod (skewer) or the back of a cleaver to press lengthwise in middle of the strips (Fig. 5); this will attach them securely to each other. Follow the same step for the other strips. Heat the oil for deep-frying; pick up a strip from the ends and gently stretch it to make it longer (Fig. 6). Carefully drop it into the hot oil and turn it over continuously with chopsticks until the cruller expands and turns golden brown; remove.

The hot crullers may be placed in split "Flaky Sesame Flat Breads" ("Shau Bing") or served with "Salty or Sweet Soy Bean Milk".

Alum may be omitted if it is unavailable.

鹹豆漿

● 備中型湯碗一個，放入適量之油條、蝦米、榨菜、葱、香菜、肉鬆及黑醋、辣油、醬油、麻油、塩等，冲入滾開的豆漿即成。

■ 豆漿做法參照第79頁「甜豆漿」，但不需加糖。

Salty Soybean Milk ("Do Jiang")

● Place the crispy Chinese crullers, dried shrimp, Szechuan pickled mustard green, green onions, coriander, pork sung, vinegar, chili oil, soy sauce, sesame oil and salt in a medium size bowl. Pour the boil soybean milk into the bowl and serve.

■ See p. 79, "Sweet Soybean Milk", for directions to make soybean milk. Dot not add sugar.

蘋果····················3 個

蛋糊 { 太白粉、麵粉···各 6 大匙
水····················2 大匙
蛋····················2 個

糖····················¾ 杯

芝麻··················1 大匙

❶備碗 1 只，將蛋糊用料在碗內調成糊狀。

❷蘋果去皮，切塊，倒入蛋糊內使每塊蘋果沾裹均勻，以中火炸 1½ 分鐘撈起，再將油燒開，蘋果回鍋炸至金黃色時撈出。

❸油 2 大匙燒熱，中火將糖下鍋炒（圖 1），邊炒邊攪至糖溶化成淡黃色透明糖汁（圖 2. 3. ），離火加入芝麻，隨即倒入炸好蘋果翻拌，即可盛入已抹油之盤內。

■上桌時附上冰水 1 小碗，吃時沾上冰水香脆可口。

■可依個人喜歡選不同的材料來做，如蕃薯、香蕉、芋頭、洋芋、山藥等。

Candied Apple Fritters
Serves 6

3 apples

Egg batter { 6 T. each: cornstarch, flour
2 T. water
2 eggs

¾ c. sugar
1 T. sesame seeds

❶ Mix the egg batter.

❷ Pare and core the apples; cut them into pieces. Place the apples in a bowl; pour the batter over the apples and mix well. Deep-fry the coated apples over medium heat for 1½ minutes; remove the apples and retain the oil. Bring the oil to a boil. Fry the apples again until golden; remove the apples.

❸ Heat the pan then add 2 T. oil; add the sugar (Fig. 1). The sugar will become golden and coarse (Fig. 2). Stir until the sugar is dissolved and the glaze becomes a golden color and transparent (Fig. 3) remove from heat. Add sesame seeds and the apples into the glaze; stir to coat the apples with the glaze. Remove the apples and place them on a lightly oiled serving plate; serve.

■ Dip the apples in ice water before eating to make them crispier and tastier.

■ Sweet potatoes, bananas, taro roots or potatoes may be substituted for the apples.

洋菜（圖 4）·············7 公克

水····················6 杯

糖····················1 杯

濃縮奶水（1 罐）··········1½ 杯

杏仁精················1 大匙

水果罐················1 小罐

● 洋菜剪段，洗淨置鍋內，加水泡約 30 分鐘（圖 5），燒沸，繼續燒至洋菜完全溶化時，加糖燒開，隨入奶水及杏仁精即熄火，盛入小碗內（圖 6）待涼凝固，可加水果一齊供食。

Sweet Almond-flavored Jello and Fruit
Serves 12

¼ oz. agar agar*(洋菜)
6 c. water
1 c. sugar
1½ c. evaporated milk
1 T. almond extract
1 16 oz. can fruit (individual preference)

● Cut agar-agar into pieces then rinse it. Place the agar-agar in a sauce pan. Add 6 cups water; and soak it for 30 minutes (Fig. 5). Heat the agar-agar over medium heat until it dissolves. Add the sugar and bring it to a boil. Add the milk and almond extract; stir and turn off the heat. Pour the liquid into individual serving bowls (Fig. 6). Allow to cool then refrigerate until the liquid sets. Add fruit before serving.

＊ Agar-agar may be purchased at most Chinese Markets. If unavailable, use gelatin and follow directions on package.

雞　捲　6捲

①	魚漿、絞肉‥‥‥‥各6兩	皮：豆腐皮‥‥‥‥‥‥6張
	洋葱(切碎)‥‥‥‥‥1杯	(15公分×20公分)
	紅蘿蔔(切碎)‥‥‥½杯	「炸油」‥‥‥‥‥‥‥適量

②	太白粉‥‥‥2大匙　糖‥1½大匙
	料酒‥‥‥‥1大匙　麻油‥1小匙
	塩‥‥‥‥‥⅓小匙　胡椒‥¼小匙

❶餡：將①、②料仔細拌勻成餡，分成六等份。

❷每張腐皮，放上一份餡，捲成長條狀(圖1.2.3.)。

❸「炸油」燒熱，放入雞捲用小火炸4分鐘，再改大火炸2分鐘至皮酥肉熟撈出。食用時可切小段，沾番茄醬、海鮮醬或醬油等。

■如無腐皮，可用煎蛋皮、紫菜或春捲皮等來代替。

龍鳳腿　18個

餡：①、②料同「雞捲」	竹簽‥‥‥‥‥‥‥‥18支
網油‥‥‥‥‥‥‥6兩	「炸油」‥‥‥‥‥‥適量

❶餡：將①、②料仔細拌勻成餡，分成18份。

❷網油切每7公分四方塊。每小張網油，放上一份餡，中間置竹簽，包成雞腿狀。油燒熱，入龍鳳腿以中火炸6分鐘至肉熟呈金黃色撈出。

■若無網油，亦可沾裹太白粉或麵包粉油炸。

> 市面所售魚漿多已加塩調味，故加②料時應注意鹹度。

蠔油腐皮捲　18個

①	里肌肉‥‥‥‥‥‥6兩	皮：豆腐皮‥‥‥‥‥6張
	蝦仁‥‥‥‥‥‥‥3兩	「炸油」‥‥‥‥‥‥適量
	肥肉‥‥‥‥‥‥‥1兩	

②	糖‥‥‥‥‥‥‥‥2小匙
	太白粉、麻油、料酒‥‥‥
	各1小匙
	塩‥‥‥‥‥‥‥‥¾小匙
	胡椒‥‥‥‥‥‥‥¼小匙

④	水‥‥‥‥‥‥‥‥1杯
	蠔油‥‥‥‥‥‥‥1大匙
	太白粉‥‥‥‥‥‥½大匙
	糖‥‥‥‥‥‥‥‥1小匙

③	香菜末‥‥‥‥‥‥⅓杯
	葱末‥‥‥‥‥‥‥2大匙

❶餡：將①料切丁，調入②料攪拌至有黏性，再加③料拌勻成餡，分18份。

❷將每張腐皮切成3小張，共計18張。每小張皮放上一大匙餡(圖4)，捲成長約6公分之春捲形狀(圖5.6.)。

❸「炸油」燒熱，將腐皮捲用中火炸4分鐘呈金黃色皮脆，撈起。

❹④料燒開，放入炸熟之腐皮捲拌勻，待水份燒乾即可置盤供食。

■若喜食脆的腐皮捲，則可將④料燒開淋在炸好的腐皮捲上，或沾④料來吃。

Bean Curd Rolls　Makes 6

Filling:

①	½ lb. each: fish cake, ground meat	②	2 T. cronstarch
	1 c. choppod onion		1½ T. sugar
	½ c. chopped carrot		1 T. cooking wine
	Skin: 6 bean curd skins*(6"x8")		1 t. sesame oil
	oil		¼ t. salt
			¼ t. pepper

❶ Filling: Mix ① and ② thoroughly then divide it into 6 portions.

❷ Place 1 portion of filling on a bean curd skin; roll up the skin sheet to form a baton-like shape (Figs. 1, 2, 3). Prepare the rest of the rolls in the same manner.

❸ Heat the oil then deep-fry the rolls over low heat for 4 minutes. Turn the heat to high and fry for 2 more minutes or until the skin is crispy; remove, Cut the rolls into serving portion pieces and serve with ketchup, hoisin sauce or soy sauce.

＊ If bean curd skins are unavailable, substitute them with egg sheets, sheets of nori, or egg roll skins.

Chicken Stick Legs　Makes 18

Filling: Use the same ingredients as ①, ② of "Bean Curd Rolls'
½ lb. pork net oil, 18 wooden sticks, oil

❶ Filling: Mix ① and ② thoroughly; divide it into 18 portions.

❷ Cut pork net oil into 3-inch squares. Place one portion of filling in the center of a pork net oil square; place a stick in the middle of filling and fold pork net oil so that it encloses filling. Follow the same step for the other sticks. Heat the oil and deep-fry the chicken drumsticks over medium heat for 6 minutes; remove, drain and serve.

You may substitute nori, bean curd skin or grated bread crumbs for pork net oil and use as directed.

> Fish cake that is available in markets is already salted; therefore, add salt in ingredients ② to taste.

Stuffed Bean Skin Rolls in Oyster Sauce　Makes 18

Filling:

①	½ lb. pork loin	④	1 c. water
	¼ lb. raw, shelled shrimp		1 T. oyster sauce
	1½ oz. pork fat		½ T. cornstarch
②	2 t. sugar		1 t. sugar
	1 t. each: cornstarch, sesame oil, cooking wine
	¾ t. salt
	¼ t. pepper
③	⅓ c. chopped coriander
	2 t. chopped green onions
	6 pre-softened bean curd skins
	6 c. oil

❶ Filling: Rinse the shrimp and devein them. Dice ingredients in ①; place them in a bowl and add ②. Mix then lightly throw the ingredients against inside of mixing bowl to combine it thoroughly. Add ③ and mix well. Divide the filling into 18 portions.

❷ Cut a bean curd skin into 3 pieces; spread 1 tablespoon filling on the bean curd skin (Fig. 4). Roll the filled skin into a 2-inch roll (Figs. 5, 6). Follow the same step for the other rolls.

❸ Heat the oil until medium hot. Deep-fry the rolls for 4 minutes or until they are golden brown and crispy; remove and drain.

❹ Heat the pan then add ④; bring to a boil. Add the fried rolls and cook over high heat until the sauce is near-dry. Remove and serve.

■ For crispier rolls, bring ④ lo a boll and sprinkle it over the fried rolls or serve boiled ④ with the rolls as a dipping sauce.

餡：里肌肉‥‥‥‥‥‥4兩　　皮：蒸熟芋頭‥‥‥‥‥12兩

① { 醬油‥‥‥‥‥‥½大匙

太白粉‥‥‥‥‥1小匙

蝦仁‥‥‥‥‥‥‥‥3兩

葱花‥‥‥‥‥‥‥3大匙

③ { 豬油‥‥‥‥‥‥‥3大匙

太白粉‥‥‥‥‥‥3大匙

糖‥‥‥‥‥‥‥1大匙

塩‥‥‥‥‥‥½小匙

「炸油」‥‥‥‥‥‥適量

② {
水‥‥‥‥‥‥‥‥4大匙

醬油‥‥‥‥‥‥‥1大匙

太白粉、料酒‥‥各½大匙

糖、麻油‥‥‥各1小匙

塩‥‥‥‥‥‥‥½小匙

胡椒‥‥‥‥‥‥¼小匙
}

❶ 餡：里肌肉切小丁，加①料調勻。蝦仁亦切小丁。
油3大匙燒熱，將里肌肉、蝦仁炒熟，加②料及葱花
拌勻，冰涼備用。

❷ 皮：蒸熟芋頭，趁熱放在板上，用刀面壓爛，加入③
料揉勻，搓長條，分切為12小塊。

❸ 每塊芋頭按扁（圖1）（黏手時撒些太白粉）將肉餡一份
放在當中捏合（圖2）即成芋餃。「炸油」燒熱，放入芋
餃大火炸3分鐘呈金黃色即成。

■「炸油」需保持高溫芋餃才不致散開，故炸時宜分數次
炸，以免溫度下降。

■芋頭若包上豆沙餡，搓成棗狀，即成芋棗（圖3）。

紅心蕃薯（地瓜）‥‥‥‥1½斤

水‥‥‥‥‥‥‥‥‥‥‥4杯

① {
水‥‥‥‥‥‥‥‥‥2杯

麥芽糖或蜂蜜‥‥‥‥1杯

檸檬汁或醋‥‥‥½大匙

塩‥‥‥‥‥‥‥¼小匙
}

❶ 蕃薯去皮洗淨，切條（圖4），加水4杯燒煮7分鐘，
倒掉湯汁，加入①料（圖5）。

❷ 蓋鍋小火煮25分鐘至蕃薯熟，糖水成糖漿時（約半杯，
如水份太多可開大火略燒乾）（圖6），將蕃薯盛盤，淋
上糖漿即成。

■食用時，可撒上適量花生粉，更為可口。

Fried Taro Turnovers　Makes 12

Filling:

①
- ⅓ lb. pork loin
- ½ T. soy sauce
- 1 t. cornstarch

- ¼ lb. raw, shelled shrimp
- 3 T. chopped green onions

③
- 3 T. lard or margarine
- 3 T. cornstarch
- 1 t. sugar
- ½ t. salt

oil

②
- 4 T. water
- 1 T. soy sauce
- ½ T. each: cornstarch, cooking wine
- 1 t. each: sugar, sesame oil
- ½ t. salt
- ¼ t. pepper

Skin: peeled taro root

❶ Filling: Dice the pork loin and mix it with ①. Rinse and
devein the shrimp, drain and dice it. Heat the pan then
add 3 t. oil. Separately stir-fry the pork and shrimp until
color changes; add green onions and ②. Toss lightly to
mix together and remove.

❷ Skin: Cut the taro slices, ⅓-inch thick. Steam the taro slices
for 30 minutes or until they are soft; keep covered.
Remove the taro slices and mash them while they are
hot. Mix with ③ and knead it into a smooth mixture. Roll
the mixture into a long roll and cut into 12 pieces.

❸ Roll a piece of taro into a ball (add cornstarch if too
moist). Flatten the ball with the palm of the hand into a
circular shape; place 1 portion (¹⁄₁₂) filling in the center and
fold in half. Pinch the edges to seal (Fig. 2). Make the
other turnovers in the same manner. Heat the oil for
deep frying; drop the turnovers into hot oil and deep-fry
for 1 minute over medium heat. Turn the heat to high and
cook for 3 minutes; remove and drain. Serve.

Keep the temperature of the oil high so that the turnovers
will not break during frying. To keep the heat high, deep-
fry 3 or 4 taro at a time.

Filling may be substituted with red bean paste (Fig. 3).

Candied Sweet Potatoes (Yams)

- 2 lbs. sweet potatoes
- 4 c. water

①
- 2 c. water
- 1 c. honey or maltose
- ½ T. lemon juice or vinegar
- ¼ t. salt

❶ Peel the potatoes and cut them into narrow wedges,
about ½ inch thick (Fig. 4). Bring 4 cups water and
potatoes to a boil; cook for 7 minutes over medium
heat; remove and drain. Add ① (Fig. 5).

❷ Cover and cook the potatoes over low heat for 25
minutes until they are tender and the syrup has been
reduced to about ½ cup (Fig. 6). Remove the potatoes
to a serving plate and pour the remaining syrup on
top. Serve.

■ When serving, sprinkle a few crushed peanuts on top
for extra flavor, if desired.

土司麵包	…………1 節	②	水	…………1 ½杯
細砂糖	…………½杯		糖	…………4 大匙
①	蛋	…………3 個		鮮乳	…………¼杯
	鮮乳	…………1 杯	③	太白粉	…………1 大匙
	猪油	…………3 大匙		水	…………1 ½大匙
	香草片(壓碎)	…………1 片	模型	…………1 個
			固體奶油或猪油	…………1 大匙

❶土司去四周硬皮，用清水浸約5分鐘取出，擠乾水份（圖1），先加入細砂糖用手搓勻（圖2），然後把①料放入，全部攪勻，倒入已抹油之布丁模型內（圖3），大火蒸40分鐘。

❷蒸熟布丁，反扣在盤上，將②料燒開，以③料勾汁，淋在布丁上即成。

■此甜點可依個人喜好，加上新鮮蘋果、葡萄干，即成水果奶油布丁。布丁四周的罐頭水果隨意。

Steamed Bread Pudding

12 servings

½ lb. bread
1½ c. contectioners sugar
① { 3 eggs
1 c. milk
3 T. shortening or lard
1 t. vanilla extract
② { 1½ c. water
4 T. granulated sugar
¼ c. milk
③ { 1 T. cornstarch } mix
1½ T. water
1 mold
1 T. butter or shortening

❶ Trim crust from bread. Soak the bread in water for 5 minutes; remove and squeeze out the water (Fig. 1). Add the confectioners sugar to the bread and knead with hand to mix well (Fig. 2). Add ① and mix. Put the soaked bread mixture into the mold (Fig. 3) and steam it over high heat for 40 minutes, remove from heat.

❷ Place a serving dish on the bowl; hold them together and invert them to remove the pudding. Bring ② to a boil; add mixture ③ to thicken then pour it over the pudding. Serve.

■ To make fruit steamed bread pudding, add fresh apples and raisins to the bread before mixing. Peaches or other canned fruit may be added as a garnish.

蒸熟芋頭	…………1 斤	豆沙	…………2 兩
	白糖	…………半斤	玻璃紙	…………1 張
	猪油	…………¼杯	猪油	…………1 大匙
①	冬瓜糖(切碎)	…………2 兩	②	花生粉	…………1 杯
	桔子餅(切碎)	…………2 兩		細砂糖	…………3 大匙
	炸香紅葱頭	…………2 大匙	蒸碗(直徑17公分)	…………1 個

❶蒸熟芋頭，趁熱壓成泥狀，加入①料攪拌均勻備用。

❷中碗內置1張玻璃紙（抹油），再把攪勻的芋泥⅔放入成凹形，中間放豆沙，將剩餘之⅓芋泥鋪滿，入鍋蒸約20分鐘，即可反扣在盤上（圖4. 5. 6.），拿掉玻璃紙。

❸將②料拌勻，洒在蒸好的芋屯四周即成。

■為增加美觀，留少許冬瓜糖及桔子餅，先放入舖上玻璃紙的蒸碗內再放入芋泥等。

Sweet Taro Cake

12 servings

1⅓ lbs. taro roots
① {
⅔ lb. granulated sugar
¼ c. shortening or lard
3 oz. chopped candied winter melon
3 oz. chopped candied orange peel } (see ■ below)
2 T. fried shallots
3 oz. red bean paste*
1 sheet plastic wrap
② {
1 T. shortening or lard
1 c. crushed peanuts
3 T. confectioners sugar
1 bowl, 8" diameter

❶ Peel and slice the taro roots; steam them until tender. Mash the taro roots while they are still hot. Add ① to the taro roots and stir until mixed well.

❷ Grease the plastic wrap with oil then line the bowl with the plastic wrap. Put ⅔ of the taro mixture in the bowl. Pack the taro firmly so that it covers the sides of the bowl. Leave an indentation in the middle of the taro; fill the center with bean paste and add the rest of the taro to cover the bean paste. Steam the taro over high heat for 20 minutes; remove. Place a serving dish on the bowl (Fig. 4), hold them together and invert them to remove the taro from the bowl (Figs. 5, 6). Remove the plastic wrap.

❸ Mix ② well then sprinkle it over the taro mold. Serve.

■ To garnish, place portion of the chopped candied winter melon and candied orange peel in the bowl before putting in the taro mixture.

✳ To make bean paste, see p. 13.

韭菜合子　　10個

餡：韭菜……………………半斤　　　塩…………………1小匙
　　粉絲……………………1把　　　　味精………………½小匙
　　蝦皮……………………半兩　　①麻油………………2大匙
　　豆腐干(大)……………1塊　　　　胡椒………………½小匙
皮：麵粉……………………2杯　　　　太白粉……………1大匙
　　滾水……………………½杯
　　冷水……………………¼杯
　　油………………………½杯

❶皮：麵粉盛入盆内，倒入滾水混合拌匀，即爲「燙麵」
　續加入¼杯冷水拌匀，揉成軟硬適度，十分光滑之麵
　糰，分切成10小塊，並擀成直徑10公分之圓薄片待用。
❷餡：蝦皮炒香，粉絲(泡軟)、韭菜、豆腐干分別切碎
　（圖1.2.3.）並調上①料拌匀，即爲餡。
❸將餡置圓薄片中央，逐塊對摺成半圓形，即成合子。
❹平底鍋入油½杯，燒熱，下合子以小火煎至兩面呈金
　黃色皮酥，餡熱即成。

Leek Turnovers　　Makes 10

Filling:
- ⅔ lb. leeks
- 2 oz. bean threads
- ⅔ oz. dried shrimp
- 1 large pressed bean curd

Skin:
- 2 c. flour
- ½ c. boiling water
- ¼ c. cold water
- ½ c. oil

①
- 1 t. salt
- 2 T. sesame oil
- ½ t. pepper
- 1 T. cornstarch

❶ Dough: Put the flour in a bowl. Add boiling water to the flour and mix well; add ¼ cup cold water and mix again. Knead the dough until smooth and elastic. Cut the dough into 10 pieces. Use a rolling pin to roll each piece of dough into a 4" circle.

❷ Filling: Stir-fry the dried shrimp until fragrant. Soak the bean threads in water until they are soft. Chop the bean threads (Fig. 1), leeks (Fig. 2), and pressed bean curd (Fig. 3); mix them with the dried shrimp and ①.

❸ Place 1 portion of the filling in the center of a dough circle. Fold the dough in half. Press edges together to enclose filling. Follow the same step to make other turnovers.

❹ Heat the pan then add ½ cup oil. Fry the turnovers on both sides over low heat until they are golden brown and the skin is crispy; remove and serve.

地瓜粿糯　　20個

紅心地瓜…………………1斤
糯米粉……………………半斤
豆沙………………………半斤
椰子粉……………………5兩

❶將地瓜去皮，洗淨，切1公分厚片（圖4），入蒸鍋（圖5）
　蒸熟置盆，趁熱壓成泥狀（圖6），加上糯米粉混合揉
　匀，成糯米糰，分成20小塊。
❷豆沙分成20個，將糯米糰包上豆沙，壓扁約1.5公分
　厚的圓薄片餅。
❸水滾後放入餅，煮至浮出水面約1分鐘，撈出，分別
　沾上椰子粉即成。
■豆沙做法參照第13頁。

Yam and Glutinous Rice Cake　　Makes 20

- 1⅓ lbs. fresh yams
- ⅔ lb. glutinous rice flour
- ⅔ lb. red bean paste*
- 7 oz. crushed coconut

❶ Peel the yams then rinse them. Cut the yams into slices, ½" thick (Fig. 4). Steam them (Fig. 5) for 20 minutes or until cooked; remove. Put the steamed yams in a bowl then mash them (Fig. 6). Add glutinous rice flour to the yams and mix well; divide the mixture into 20 portions.

❷ Divide the bean paste into 20 portions. Place one portion of the bean paste in the center of a rice dough; wrap the rice dough to enclose the filling. Flatten the rice dough into a round circle, ⅜" thick. Follow the same step for the other portions.

❸ Bring water in a pot to a boil. Put the dough circles in water and cook for 1 minute; remove. Coat the cakes with crushed coconut.

＊ See p. 13 for direction to make bean paste.

椒鹽月餅　20個

<table>
<tr><td rowspan="7">①</td><td>館</td><td>熟麵粉‥‥‥‥‥‥‥‥‥2杯</td></tr>
</table>

館｛
熟麵粉‥‥‥‥‥‥‥‥‥2杯
糖粉‥‥‥‥‥‥‥‥‥1½杯
黑芝麻粉‥‥‥‥‥‥‥2½杯
① 核桃‥‥‥‥‥‥‥‥‥‥2兩
花椒粉‥‥‥‥‥‥‥‥1小匙
鹽‥‥‥‥‥‥‥‥‥‥2小匙
豬油‥‥‥‥‥‥‥‥‥‥1杯
黑芝麻‥‥‥‥‥‥‥‥‥‥‥2兩

油酥皮：
麵粉‥‥‥‥‥‥‥‥‥2杯
② 豬油‥‥‥‥‥‥‥‥‥5大匙
水‥‥‥‥‥‥‥‥‥10大匙
鹽‥‥‥‥‥‥‥‥‥¼小匙
③ 麵粉‥‥‥‥‥‥‥‥‥1杯
豬油‥‥‥‥‥‥‥‥‥5大匙

❶館：核桃（圖1）以牙籤去膜（圖2）以趕麵棍壓碎（圖3）備用。

❷將①料置盆內拌勻成糰，並分成20份。

❸油酥皮：參照第25頁「臘味蘿蔔餅」做法❷，做成油酥皮，共做20份。

❹將做好油酥皮，趕成直徑8公分，中間稍厚的圓形麵皮，包上館，並用手輕壓成扁圓形（厚約1.5公分），塗上少許水，再沾上黑芝蘇置烤盤，將烤箱燒熱至350°F烤20分鐘即成。

■熟麵粉：將麵粉攤開，置鋁盤內，蒸15分鐘或以300°F烤15分鐘，如使用生麵粉，覺黏膩、夾口。

Szechuan Peppercorn Salt Moon Cakes

Makes 20

Filling:
① {
2　c.　steamed or cooked flour*
1½　c.　confectioners sugar
2½　c.　crushed black sesame seeds
3　oz.　walnuts (Fig. 1)
1　t.　Szechuan peppercorn powder
2　t.　salt
1　c.　shortening or pork fat
}
Skin:
② {
2　c.　flour
5　T.　shortening or pork fat
10　T.　water
¼　t.　salt
}
③ {
1　c.　flour
5　T.　shortening or pork fat
}
3　oz.　black sesame seeds

❶ Remove the skin of the walnut with a toothpick (Fig. 2). Crush the walnuts (Fig. 3).
❷ Filling: Mix ① in a bowl; divide it into 20 portions.
❸ Dough: See p. 25, Turnip Cakes, step ❷.
❹ Preheat oven to 350°F. Use a rolling pin to roll a piece of dough into a 3″ circle. The edges should be thinner than the middle. Place 1 portion of the filling in the center of the dough circle; wrap the dough to enclose the filling. Lightly flatten the dough circle with the palm of the hand so that the cake is ⅜″ thick. Follow the same step to make other cakes. Lightly brush the cakes with water then coat them with black sesame seeds. Place the cakes on a baking pan and bake them in preheated 350°F oven for 20 minutes; remove and serve.
✱ Spread the flour in a pan then bake the flour at 300°F for 15 minutes. The cake will be sticky if the steaming or baking procedure is omitted.

綠豆凸餅　20個

館｛綠豆沙‥‥‥‥‥‥‥‥2斤
紅葱頭末‥‥‥‥‥‥2大匙
絞肉‥‥‥‥‥‥‥‥3兩
① 咖哩粉‥‥‥‥‥‥‥1大匙
鹽‥‥‥‥‥‥‥‥‥½小匙
糖‥‥‥‥‥‥‥‥‥1小匙
食用紅色水‥‥‥‥‥‥‥‥適量

油酥皮：
麵粉‥‥‥‥‥‥‥‥‥2杯
② 豬油‥‥‥‥‥‥‥‥‥5大匙
水‥‥‥‥‥‥‥‥‥10大匙
鹽‥‥‥‥‥‥‥‥‥¼小匙
③ 麵粉‥‥‥‥‥‥‥‥‥1杯
豬油‥‥‥‥‥‥‥‥‥5大匙

❶館：將①料依序炒香拌勻成肉館，待涼（圖4）。

❷油酥皮：參照第25頁「臘味蘿蔔餅」做法❷，做成油酥皮，共做20份。

❸綠豆沙分成20份，並分別包入肉館（圖5），即為豆沙館。

❹將做好的油酥皮，壓成直徑8公分，中間稍厚的圓形麵皮，包上豆沙館，用手輕壓成扁圓形（厚約1.5公分），中央並用手掌壓成凹狀（圖6），以筷子沾食用紅色水在面上點三點，排在烤盤上，烤箱燒熱至350°F，烤約20分鐘即成。

Green Bean Paste Cakes

Makes 20

Filling:
2⅔ lbs. green bean paste
① {
2　T.　chopped shallots
¼　lb.　ground beef or pork
1　T.　curry powder
½　t.　salt
1　t.　sugar
}
Skin:
② {
2　c.　flour
5　T.　shortening or pork fat
10　T.　water
¼　t.　salt
}
③ {
1　c.　flour
5　T.　shortening or pork fat
}
red food coloring

❶ Stir-fry ①, as listed, until mixed well; remove and allow to cool (Fig. 4).
❷ Dough: See p. 25, Turnip Cakes, step ❷.
❸ Filling: Divide the green bean paste into 20 portions. Put 1 portion (½₀) of ① in the center of the paste (Fig. 5); wrap the paste to enclose the filling. Follow the same step for the other portions.
❹ Preheat oven to 350°F. Use a rolling pin to roll a dough into 3″ circle. Make the edges thinner than the middle. Place 1 portion of the filling on the center of the dough circle; wrap the dough to enclose the filling. Lightly flatten the dough with the palm of the hand so that the cake is 3″ thick. Press the center of the dough to make a concave shape (Fig. 6). Follow the same step to make other cakes. Lightly dip the tip of a chopstick in red food coloring then stamp three dots on the surface of each cake. Bake the cakes in preheated 350°F oven for 20 minutes; remove and serve.

餡：絞肉⋯⋯⋯⋯⋯⋯⋯4兩　　油酥皮：
蝦仁⋯⋯⋯⋯⋯⋯⋯半斤
韭黃⋯⋯⋯⋯⋯⋯⋯6兩
　　　{ 塩⋯⋯⋯⋯⋯⋯1小匙　　　②{ 麵粉⋯⋯⋯⋯⋯2杯
① { 味精⋯⋯⋯⋯⋯1小匙　　　　　{ 猪油⋯⋯⋯⋯⋯5大匙
　　{ 胡椒⋯⋯⋯⋯⋯½小匙　　　　　{ 水⋯⋯⋯⋯⋯10大匙
　　{ 麻油⋯⋯⋯⋯⋯1小匙　　　　　{ 塩⋯⋯⋯⋯⋯¼小匙
　　　　　　　　　　　　　　　③{ 麵粉⋯⋯⋯⋯⋯1杯
　　　　　　　　　　　　　　　　{ 猪油⋯⋯⋯⋯⋯5大匙

❶餡：將絞肉、蝦仁分別切碎，韭黃切小段，與①料拌
　匀成餡，並分成20份。
❷油酥皮：參照第25頁「臘味蘿蔔餅」做法❷，做成油酥
　皮，共做20份。
❸將做好油酥皮，趕成直徑8公分，中間稍厚的圓形麵
　皮，包上餡，捏成三角形，呈鴨掌狀（圖1. 2. 3. ）。
❹油半鍋燒熱，以小火將做好的鴨掌炸約8分鐘至熟即
　成，或以烤箱燒熱至375°F 烤20分鐘亦可。
■花邊捏法參考第25頁咖哩酥餃做法❸。

Triangular-shaped Buns

Makes 20

Filling:
⅓ lb. ground beef or pork
⅔ lb. raw, shelled shrimp
½ lb. yellow Chinese chives
① { 1 t. salt
　{ ½ t. pepper
　{ 1 t. sesame oil
Skin:
② { 2 c. flour
　{ 5 T. shortening or pork fat
　{ 10 T. water
　{ ¼ t. salt
③ { 1 c. flour
　{ 5 T. shortening or pork fat
oil

❶ Filling: Chop the ground beef and shrimp. Cut the chives into small pieces; add to ① and mix well. Divide the filling into 20 portions.
❷ Dough: See p. 25, Turnip Cakes, step ❷.
❸ Use a rolling pin to roll a piece of dough into 3" circle; make the edges thinner than the middle. Place 1 portion of filling in the center of the dough circle; fold the dough to form a triangle (Fig. 1) and to enclose the filling (Fig. 2). Pleat the edges* (Fig. 3).
❹ Heat the oil for deep-frying. Deep-fry the buns over low heat for 8 minutes or until cooked. Or preheat the oven to 375°F and bake the buns for 20 minutes.
✱ To pleat edges, see p. 25, Curry Meat Turnovers, step ❸

餡：豆沙半斤⋯⋯⋯⋯1杯　　油酥皮：
鹹蛋黃⋯⋯⋯⋯⋯⋯20個
生蛋黃⋯⋯⋯⋯⋯⋯1個
　　　　　　　　　　　　　　①{ 麵粉⋯⋯⋯⋯⋯1杯
　　　　　　　　　　　　　　　{ 猪油⋯⋯⋯⋯⋯3大匙
　　　　　　　　　　　　　　　{ 水⋯⋯⋯⋯⋯4大匙
　　　　　　　　　　　　　　　{ 塩⋯⋯⋯⋯⋯⅛小匙
　　　　　　　　　　　　　　②{ 麵粉⋯⋯⋯⋯⋯1杯
　　　　　　　　　　　　　　　{ 猪油⋯⋯⋯⋯⋯5大匙

❶鹹蛋黃以清水洗淨，置烤盤，入烤箱以300°F 烤約10
　分鐘至熟。
❷豆沙分成20份，取1份豆沙包上一個蛋黃（圖4）待用。
❸油酥皮：參照第25頁「臘味蘿蔔餅」做法❷，做成油酥
　皮，共做20份。
❹將做好的油酥皮趕成直徑4公分，中間稍厚的圓形麵
　皮，包上豆沙蛋黃（圖5. 6. ），表面塗蛋液，置烤盤，
　烤箱燒熱至350°F 烤約20分鐘至熟即成。

Egg-yolk Rolls

Makes 20

Filling:
{ 1 c. bean paste
{ 20 salted egg yolks
Skin:
① { 1 c. flour
　{ 3 T. shortening or pork fat
　{ 4 T. water
　{ ⅛ t. salt
② { 1 c. flour
　{ 5 T. shortening or pork fat
1 beaten egg yolk

❶ Rinse the salted egg yolks then bake them at 300°F for 10 minutes or until cooked.
❷ Filling: Divide the bean paste into 20 portions. Place 1 salted egg yolk in the center of one portion of bean paste; wrap the bean paste to enclose the yolk (Fig. 4). Follow the same step for the other portions.
❸ Dough: See p.25, Turnip Cakes, step ❷.
❹ Preheat the oven to 350°F. Use a rolling pin to roll a dough piece into a 2" circle; make the edges thinner than the center. Place 1 portion of filling in the center of the dough circle (Fig. 5); wrap to enclose the filling (Fig. 6). Follow the same step to make other rolls. Brush the top of the rolls with beaten egg yolk. Bake the rolls in preheated 350°F oven for 20 minutes or until cooked; remove and serve.

蛋 塔　20個

餡：

① ⎧ 糖‥‥‥‥‥‥‥‥‥‥1杯
⎪ 熱水‥‥‥‥‥‥‥‥1¼杯
⎪ 奶粉‥‥‥‥‥‥‥‥2大匙
⎪ 塩‥‥‥‥‥‥‥‥‥¼小匙
⎩ 香草片‥‥‥‥‥‥‥少許
蛋‥‥‥‥‥‥‥‥‥‥‥5個
蛋塔模型‥‥‥‥‥‥‥‥20個

油酥皮：

② ⎧ 麵粉‥‥‥‥‥‥‥‥2杯
⎪ 豬油‥‥‥‥‥‥‥‥5大匙
⎪ 水‥‥‥‥‥‥‥‥‥10大匙
⎩ 塩‥‥‥‥‥‥‥‥‥¼小匙
③ ⎧ 麵粉‥‥‥‥‥‥‥‥1杯
⎩ 豬油‥‥‥‥‥‥‥‥5大匙

❶油酥皮：參照第25頁「臘味蘿蔔餅」做法❷做成油酥皮共做20份。

❷將做好的油酥皮趕成直徑8公分，中間稍厚的圓形薄皮，放入塔模內（圖1），輕輕上下抖動讓麵皮與模型疊合（圖2）同時順邊緣捏成花邊（圖3）花邊捏法參考第25頁咖哩酥餃做法❸。

❸蛋打散，倒入調好的①料內拌勻過濾，分裝注入20個塔模，置烤盤，移入烤箱下層，將烤箱燒熱至350°F烤約25分鐘即可。

Egg Pudding　Makes 20

Filling:

① ⎧ 1　c. sugar
⎪ 1¼　c. hot water
⎪ 2　t. milk powder
⎪ ¼　t. salt
⎩ vanilla extract
5　eggs

Skin:

② ⎧ 2　c. flour
⎪ 5　T. shortening or pork fat
⎪ 10　T. water
⎩ ¼　t. salt
③ ⎧ 1　c. flour
⎩ 5　T. shortening or pork fat
20　molds

❶ Skin: See p. 25, Turnip Cakes, step ❷.
❷ Use a rolling pin to roll the skin into a 3″ circle; make the edges thinner than the center. Put the dough circle in a mold (Fig. 1). Lightly shake the mold and arrange the dough to line on the mold (Fig. 2). Pleat the edges (see p. 25, Turnip Cakes, step ❸).
❸ Preheat oven to 350°F. Beat the eggs. Pour ① into the eggs and mix well; strain. Pour the strained mixture into molds. Bake for 25 minutes; remove and serve.

椰茸金露酥　20個

① ⎧ 椰子粉‥‥‥‥‥‥‥4杯
⎪ 奶油‥‥‥‥‥‥‥‥½杯
⎪ 蛋黃‥‥‥‥‥‥‥‥2個
⎩ 煉奶(大)‥‥‥‥‥‥¾罐
② ⎧ 麵粉‥‥‥‥‥‥‥‥1¼杯
⎪ 奶粉‥‥‥‥‥‥‥‥3大匙
⎪ 發粉‥‥‥‥‥‥‥‥¼小匙
⎩ 香草片‥‥‥‥‥‥‥1片

③ ⎧ 奶油‥‥‥‥‥‥‥‥½杯
⎪ 糖‥‥‥‥‥‥‥‥‥¼杯
⎩ 蛋‥‥‥‥‥‥‥‥‥1個
④ ⎧ 蛋黃‥‥‥‥‥‥‥‥2個
⎩ 奶油(液體)‥‥‥‥‥1大匙
蛋塔模型‥‥‥‥‥‥‥‥20個

❶將①料拌勻成餡，分成20個小麵糰，並將④料拌合。

❷②料過篩置盆，加入③料混合倒出拌勻（圖4）成麵糰，分成20小塊。

❸將小麵糰放入模型內（圖5），用手按壓成形（圖6），並將餡分裝入做好之模型裏，移入烤箱下層，以350°F烤約25分鐘，取出，迅速塗上④料，使表面光亮、美觀，即成。

Coconut Tarts　Makes 20

① ⎧ 4　c. shredded coconut
⎪ ½　c. butter
⎪ 2　egg yolk
⎩ 9　oz. evaporated milk
② ⎧ 1¼　c. flour
⎪ 3　T. milk powder
⎪ ¼　t. baking powder
⎩ 1　t. vanilla extract
③ ⎧ ½　c. butter
⎪ ¼　c. sugar
⎩ 1　egg
④ ⎧ 2　egg yolk ⎫ mix
⎩ 1　T. melted butter ⎭
20　molds

❶ Skin: Mix ① well then divide it into 20 portions.
❷ Sift ② then place it in a bowl. Add ③ to ② and mix well; remove and knead the dough until it is smooth (Fig. 4). Divide the dough into 20 portions.
❸ Preheat oven to 350°F. Place a piece of dough in a mold (Fig. 5). Press the dough to line the mold (Fig. 6). Put 1 portion of the filling into the dough mold. Follow the same step to make the other tarts. Bake the tarts for 25 minutes; remove and brush ④ on top of them immediately. Serve.

栗子糊 8人份

乾栗子仁·····················半斤
水························3杯
① { 冰糖·····················1杯
　　水······················1杯

❶乾栗子仁（圖1）泡水約24小時（圖2），以牙籤去膜（圖3），加水煮30分鐘至爛，並撈出待涼。

❷備果汁機，倒入處理好的栗子及水3杯，攪打成糊狀。

❸鍋內放入①料煮開，倒入栗子糊，輕輕攪勻，以小火煮，邊煮邊攪拌以免沾鍋，煮開即成。

■如選用新鮮帶殼的栗子，須先加水煮爛約半小時後，對切半，以小湯匙挖出栗子仁，即可使用。做法❷❸同上。

■如使用花生或芝蔴，可先炒或烤熟後使用。做法❷❸同上。

■食用時可酌加炸脆的餛飩皮或蘇打餅乾。

Chestnut Soup
8 servings

⅔ lb. dried, shelled chestnuts (Fig. 1)
3 c. water
① { 1 c. rock sugar
　　1 c. water

❶ Soak the chestnuts in water for 24 hours (Fig. 2). Remove the skin of the chestnuts with a toothpick (Fig. 3). Add water to the chestnuts and cook for 10 minutes until soft; remove and allow to cool.

❷ Place the chestnuts and 3 cups water in a blender; blend into smooth paste.

❸ Bring ① to a boil. Add the paste and stir to mix. Bring the mixture to a boil at low heat; stir continuously to prevent from sticking to the pan. Remove and serve.

▬ If fresh chestnuts are used, cook the chestnuts in water for 30 minutes. Cut each chestnut in half and remove the nuts with a spoon. Continue to follow step ❷ and step ❸.

▬ Fried and crushed won ton skins or crushed crackers may be added to the soup to serve.

核桃酪 8人份

核桃·····················5兩
紅棗·····················4個
水·······················2杯
① { 砂糖·····················半杯
　　水······················4杯
② { 太白粉···················3大匙
　　水·····················3大匙

❶核桃煮10分鐘至軟，去膜（參照椒塩月餅圖2），紅棗（圖4）以熱水泡軟（圖5），去籽（圖6）。

❷將核桃、紅棗及水2杯放入果汁機內攪打約10分鐘成糊狀。

❸將①料置鍋，加入核桃糊，以小火煮滾後，再以②料勾芡即成。

Sweet Walnuts Soup
8 servings

7 oz. shelled walnuts
3 oz. red dates
2 c. water
① { ½ c. brown sugar
　　4 c. water
② { 3 T. cornstarch
　　3 l. water

❶ Cook the shelled walnuts in water for 10 minutes or until soft; remove. Remove the skin of the walnut (Fig. 2 of Szechuan Peppercorn Salt Moon Cakes). Soak the red dates (Fig. 4) in hot water until soft (Fig. 5); remove the pits from the dates (Fig. 6).

❷ Place the walnuts, dates and 2 cups water in a blender; blend for 10 minutes until smooth.

❸ Place ① in a pan. Add the blended walnut mixture to ①; bring the mixture to a boil at low heat. Add ② to thicken; serve.

MORE FROM WEI-CHUAN PUBLISHING

COOKBOOKS :

ALL COOKBOOKS ARE BILINGUAL (ENGLISH/CHINESE) UNLESS FOOTNOTED OTHERWISE

Apetizers, Chinese Style
Chinese Appetizers & Garnishes
Chinese Cooking, Favorite Home Dishes
Chinese Cooking For Beginners (Rev.) [1]
Chinese Cooking Made Easy
Chinese Cuisine
Chinese Cuisine-Cantonese Style
Chinese Cuisine-Shanghai Style
Chinese Cuisine-Szechwan Style
Chinese Cuisine-Taiwanese Style
Chinese Dim Sum
Chinese Herb Cooking for Health
Chinese Home Cooking for Health
Chinese One Dish Meals (Rev.) [3]
Chinese Snacks (Rev.)
Favorite Chinese Dishes
Fish [3]

Great Garnishes
Healthful Cooking
Indian Cuisine
International Baking Delights
Japanese Cuisine
Low Cholesterol Chinese Cuisine
Mexican Cooking Made Easy [4]
Noodles, Chinese Home-Cooking
Noodles, Classical Chinese Cooking
One Dish Meals; From Popular Cuisines [3]
Rice, Chinese Home-Cooking
Rice, Traditional Chinese Cooking
Shellfish [3]
Simply Vegetarian
Thai Cooking Made Easy
Vegetarian Cooking

SMALL COOKBOOK SERIES

Beef [2]
Chicken [2]
Soup! Soup! Soup!
Tofu! Tofu! Tofu!
Vegetables [2]
Very! Very! Vegetarian!

VIDEOS

Chinese Garnishes I [5]
Chinese Garnishes II [5]
Chinese Stir-Frying: Beef [5]
Chinese Stir-Frying: Chicken [5]
Chinese Stir-Frying: Vegetables [5]

OTHERS

Carving Tools

---

1 Also available in English/Spanish, French/Chinese, and German/Chinese
2 English and Chinese are in separate editions
3 Trilingual English/Chinese/Spanish edition
4 Also available in English/Spanish
5 English Only

Wei-Chuan Cookbooks can be purchased in the U.S.A., Canada and twenty other countries worldwide
1455 Monterey Pass Road, #110, Monterey Park, CA 91754, U.S.A. • Tel: (323)261-3880 • Fax: (323) 261-3299

味全叢書

食譜系列

(如無數字標註,即為中英對照版)

美味小菜
拼盤與盤飾
實用家庭菜
實用中國菜(修訂版) [1]
速簡中國菜
中國菜
廣東菜
上海菜
四川菜

台灣菜
飲茶食譜
養生藥膳
養生家常菜
簡賢專輯(修訂版) [3]
點心專輯
家常100
魚 [3]
盤飾精選

健康食譜
印度菜
實用烘焙
日本料理
均衡飲食
墨西哥菜 [4]
麵,家常篇
麵,精華篇
簡賢(五國風味) [3]

米食,家常篇
米食,傳統篇
蝦、貝、蟹 [3]
健康素
泰國菜
素食

味全小食譜

牛肉 [2]
雞肉 [2]
蔬菜 [2]

湯
豆腐
家常素食

錄影帶

盤飾 I [5]
盤飾 II [5]

炒菜入門,牛肉 [5]
炒菜入門,雞肉 [5]
炒菜入門,蔬菜 [5]

其他

雕花刀

---

1 中英、英西、中法、中德版   2 中文版及英文版   3 中、英、西對照版   4 英西版   5 英文版

味全食譜在台、美加及全球二十餘國皆有發行 • 味全出版社有限公司 • 台北市仁愛路4段28號2樓
Tel:(02)2702-1148 • Fax:(02)2704-2729

OTROS LIBROS DE WEI-CHUAN

EDICIONES EN ESPAÑOL

Cocina China Para Principiantes, Edición Revisada [1]
Cocina Popular de Un Solo Platillo [2]
Comida China de Un Solo Platillo, Edición Revisada [2]
Comida Mexicana, Fácil de Preparar [3]
Mariscos, Estilo Chino Fácil de Preparar [2]
Pescado, Estilo Chino Fácil de Preparar [2]

---

1 Disponible en Inglés/Español, Inglés/Chino, Francés/Chino, y Alemán/Chino
2 Edición trilingüe Inglés/Chino/Español
3 Disponible en ediciones bilingües Inglés/Español e Inglés/Chino

Los Libros de Cocina Wei-Chuan se pueden comprar en E.E.U.U., Canadá y otros 20 países a través del mundo.
1455 Monterey Pass Road, #110, Monterey Park, CA 91754, U.S.A. • Tel: (323)261-3880 • Fax: (323) 261-3299

國立中央圖書館出版品預行編目資料　　台內著字第35251號

點心專輯＝Chinese snacks/黃淑惠編著．—
7版．—臺北市：味全，民80
　面：　　公分
ISBN 957-9285-05-5（平裝）

1.食譜—點心

427.16　　　　　　　　　　　　　80000769

Information listed above is for Taiwan, R.O.C. use only